TS I ENGLISH Part Viz. ENGLISH EMPIRE containing ye Articklands near Hudsons Bay New North & South Wales New Britain
Florida California Sommer Is Bahama Is Jamaica &c Cariby Is II. SPANISH P. viz N Spain of ye Antilles III. FRENCH
BAFFINS BAY
STRAITS
Straits
NEW WALES
NEW
BRADOR
NEW BRITAIN
WALES
NEW FRANCE
LAKE SUPERIOR
L PISCOUTAGAMI
L. TABITIBIS
LAKE HURONS
LAKE ERIE
PENNSYLVANIA
MARYLAND
VIRGINIA
CAROLINA
Cape Cod
The Main Bank
False Bank
SEA OF THE ENGLISH EMPIRE
Bermudas als Summer Islands
THE GOLF OR BAY OF MEXICO
BAHAMA ISLANDS
ANTILLES Is
WEST INDIAN SEA
CARIBY ISLANDS
SOTTAVAN Is
YUCATAN
JAMAICA

· VOICES · *from* COLONIAL AMERICA

MASSACHUSETTS

1620–1776

MICHAEL BURGAN

WITH

BRENDAN McCONVILLE, PH.D., CONSULTANT

NATIONAL GEOGRAPHIC

WASHINGTON, D.C.

STAFF FOR THIS BOOK

Nancy Laties Feresten, *Vice President, Editor-in-Chief of Children's Books*
Suzanne Patrick Fonda, *Project Editor*
Robert D. Johnston, Ph.D., *Associate Professor and Director, Teaching of History Program University of Illinois at Chicago, Overall Series Editor*
Bea Jackson, *Design Director, Children's Books and Education Publishing Group*
Jean Cantu, *Illustrations Specialist*
Carl Mehler, *Director of Maps*
Justin Morrill, *The M Factory, Inc., Map Research, Design, and Production*
Connie D. Binder, *Indexer*
Rebecca Hinds, *Managing Editor*
R. Gary Colbert, *Production Director*
Lewis R. Bassford, *Production Manager*
Vincent P. Ryan and Maryclare Tracy, *Manufacturing Managers*

Voices from Colonial Massachusetts was prepared by
CREATIVE MEDIA APPLICATIONS, INC.

Michael Burgan, *Writer*
Fabia Wargin Design, Inc., *Design and Production*
Matt Levine, *Editor*
Susan Madoff, *Associate Editor*
Laurie Lieb, *Copyeditor*
Jennifer Bright, *Image Researcher*

Body text is set in Deepdene, sidebars are Caslon 337 Oldstyle, and display text is Cochin Archaic Bold.

LIBRARY OF CONGRESS CATALOGING-IN-PUBLICATION DATA REQUESTED

ISBN 0-7922-6383-9 (Hardcover)
ISBN 0-7922-6599-8 (Library)

Printed in Belgium

Contents

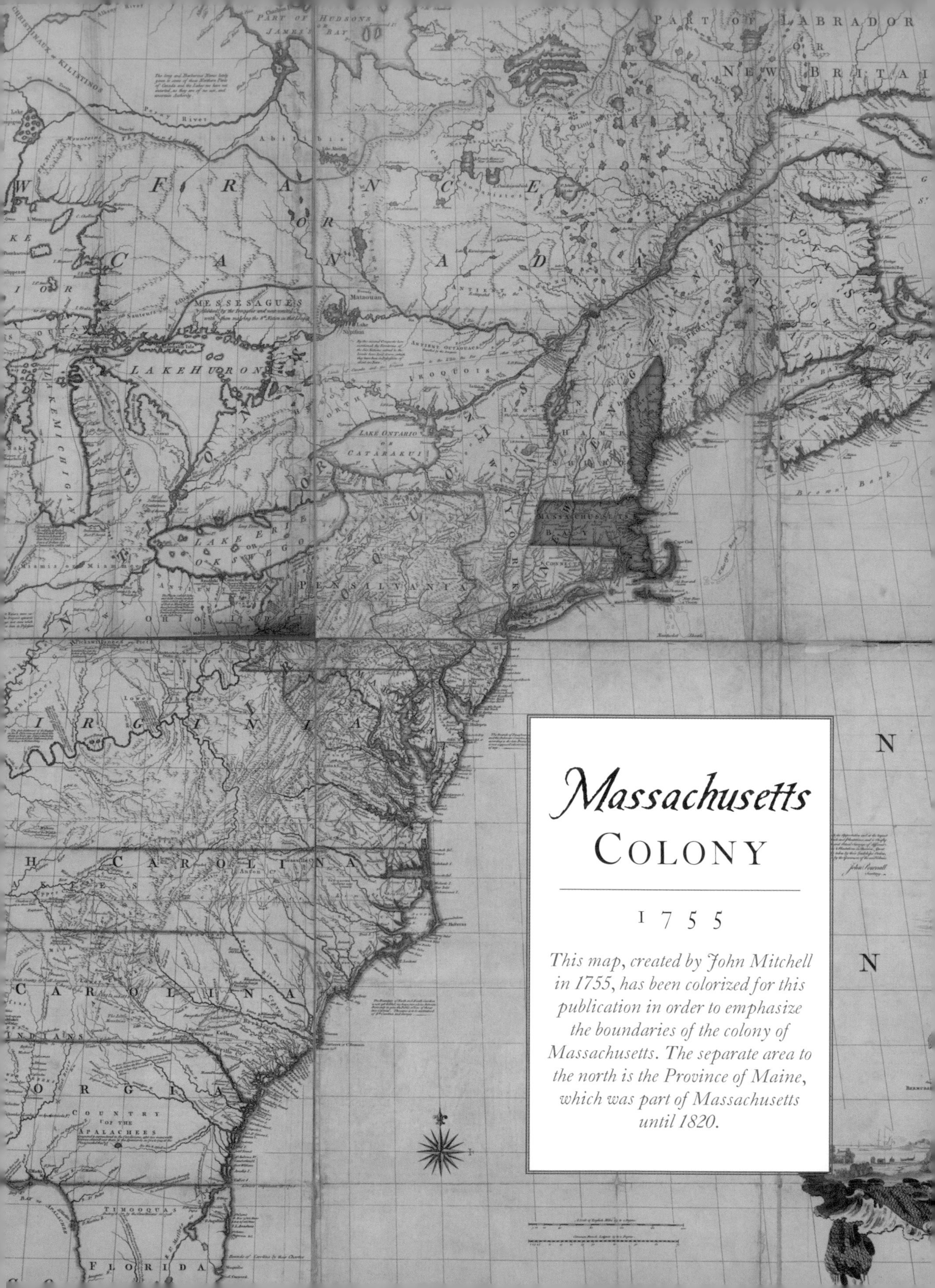

Massachusetts COLONY

1755

This map, created by John Mitchell in 1755, has been colorized for this publication in order to emphasize the boundaries of the colony of Massachusetts. The separate area to the north is the Province of Maine, which was part of Massachusetts until 1820.

Introduction

by

Brendan McConville, Ph.D.

This colored engraving shows settlers arriving for a gathering in Boston's first meeting house. The meeting house was used for religious worship and as a place to hold public debate and community celebrations.

To visit Massachusetts is, in a way, to step back in time to the distant past. You would encounter places whose names and histories can be traced to the Puritans and Pilgrims, the Wampanoag and the Shawmut. Stone walls that surround trees by the side of the road, markers and greens in the center of towns and villages—even the way people talk—all have connections with colonial times. The places—Boston, Salem, Plymouth, Cape Cod, Deerfield, and Northampton—

played a central part in this historic period, its struggles, the triumphs and tragedies. The people—John Winthrop, Anne Hutchinson, Samuel Adams, Jonathan Edwards, Solomon Stoddard, Phillis Wheatley, King Philip—have a special hold on our national imagination. They are the seeds from which our culture has somehow sprung and now grown to full bloom.

As part of the National Geographic series *Voices from Colonial America*, this volume is designed to introduce readers to the near mythic places, personalities, and events from the early history of Massachusetts. The stories that older generations of Americans know and value are retold here in light of new information that has been discovered about the colonial period. Readers gain a basic understanding of the origins of present-day communities, the bold courage and religious faith that drove the English migrations to Massachusetts, and the tragic consequences of war and disease experienced by the Native American populations as a result of the arrival of Pilgrim and Puritan settlers.

Students come to understand how the values and beliefs brought from England shaped the new society that emerged; how those same factors often led to actions that seem strange to us now; how the Puritan settlements were forced to accommodate Britain's empire in the 18th century;

OPPOSITE: This printing press, set up in Cambridge, Massachusetts, in 1638 by Stephen Daye, was the first in the 13 Colonies.

and how being part of that empire tied them to a broader world of commerce and concerns. Bitter political disputes between governors appointed by the King and the General Court (assembly) in Massachusetts often accompanied these developments as colonists began to seek greater freedom from England. Arguments over paper money, trade, religion and other issues defined political life for Massachusetts's settlers. In 1763, as the King and Parliament began to tax the colonies to refill their empty coffers, much of the population united in resistance to what they termed British tyranny. That resistance itself drew on Massachusetts's heritage and values to define the colonists' rights, beginning the process that created a distinctive American identity in the wake of the Revolutionary War.

All are part of the important and complex lessons of early Massachusetts. The voices from those distant times speak as forcefully today as they have for 300 years, and the examples offered by their lives as they struggled with change are still an essential part of the education of any young American.

CHAPTER ONE

Colonial Beginnings

THE DESIRE TO WORSHIP *as they choose leads some English citizens to move to Massachusetts.*

In the 16th and 17th centuries, European explorers and settlers sailed the Atlantic to North America. They sought to control lands in the "New World" (as Europeans called the Americas). The Europeans hoped to ship gold, furs, and other resources to the "Old World" they had left behind.

Bartholomew Gosnold was an English adventurer who sailed for the New World in 1602. On board his ship, the *Concord*, were 20 men who hoped to start a colony along

OPPOSITE: In 1602, English explorer Bartholomew Gosnold was greeted by friendly Native Americans bearing gifts as he landed upon the shores of what would later become known as Massachusetts.

the east coast of North America. In the summer of that year, Gosnold briefly explored a series of small islands, and in a letter to his father, he noted that the land had *"as healthful a climate as any."* As they explored the islands, Gosnold and his crew found sassafras, a plant that Europeans prized for its flavor in tea. However, the colonists changed their minds about staying in the New World. Their food supplies were running low, and they weren't sure they could survive, so they returned to England.

The islands Gosnold reached were part of what Europeans later called Massachusetts. The word comes from the name of an Algonquian Indian tribe that lived near present-day Boston. In the Algonquian language, Massachusetts means "great hills." For decades, European sailors had fished for cod in nearby waters and taken their catch back to Europe. However, the name "Massachusetts" would not be used regularly until the early 1630s.

In the years after Gosnold's voyage, other English colonists left for the New World. In 1607, John Smith helped found the Jamestown colony in Virginia. After two years there, he returned to England. In 1614, investors looking to start other colonies arranged for Smith to go back to North America. This time, he explored Massachusetts and lands to its north. He named part of the region he found New England.

Smith mapped the shoreline of Massachusetts and other parts of New England. Smith called one harbor

Patuxet, the name of a nearby Indian village. In England, Prince Charles, the son of King James I, renamed the harbor for the English seaport of Plymouth to make future English settlers feel more at home.

Puritans

In 1533, King Henry VIII had established a new national Church of England called the Anglican Church. Anglicans, like Catholics, thought that following the teachings of church leaders and doing good deeds were important for getting into heaven. The new church, however, was one of many new faiths created during the 16th century in protest against certain Catholic policies that had been adhered to for hundreds of years. These new faiths, including Anglican, were called Protestant religions.

An "AD" *for* NEW ENGLAND

In 1616, John Smith wrote a long article praising the land he had seen in Massachusetts and along the rest of the New England coast. Here is part of what he wrote:

The ground is so fertile that doubtless it is capable of producing any grain, fruits, or seeds you will sow or plant.... Some tender plants may not live because the summer is not very hot and the winter is colder... than we find at the same latitude in Europe or Asia. Yet, I made a garden upon the top of a rocky island... in May, that grew so well that it provided us salads in June and July.

Some members of the Church of England believed that strictly following the teachings of the Bible was more important than doing good deeds or obeying what church leaders preached. These people became known as Puritans. They said that everything a person needed to know was in the Bible and that a Christian's deep faith that Jesus Christ was the Son of God was all a person needed to get into heaven.

Puritan—a Protestant whose faith was based on the Bible rather than the teachings of church leaders

Another group of Puritans called Congregationalists believed that, in addition to strictly following the Bible, each religious community, or congregation, should be independent and make its own decisions. A third, smaller group of Puritans developed during the 1580s. These Puritans separated completely from the Church of England to worship as they chose. They became known as Separatists.

Congregationalist—a Puritan who believed that individual community church congregations should be self-governing

Separatist—a Puritan who wanted to break away completely from the Church of England

Seeking Religious Freedom

The Separatists wanted to form a new church, which was illegal. The political and religious leaders of England disliked any religious group that rejected the Anglican

Church. William Bradford, a Separatist leader, wrote that some Separatists were *"clapped in prison, others had their houses . . . watched night and day . . . and the most were [forced] to flee. . . ."*

In 1608, Bradford and a group of Separatists moved to the Netherlands. Many Dutch were fundamentalist Protestants, and they let the English newcomers worship as they chose. Not all Dutch, however, followed the Bible as closely as the Separatists did. Separatist leaders believed that the group needed to move again in order to truly live as God commanded. John Robinson, a Separatist minister, said God wanted his followers *"separated . . . from all other peoples, to call upon his name in faith and to glorify him."*

In 1617, Separatist leaders sent two men to London, England, to meet with the owners of the Virginia Company, which controlled the colony in Jamestown. The company agreed to let the Separatists settle on land near the northern boundary of Virginia. At the time, that colony stretched up to what is now southern New York. The Separatists received land close to the Hudson River in what would one day be New York and New Jersey.

THE *MAYFLOWER* SAILS TO MASSACHUSETTS

In July 1620, Bradford's small group of Separatists returned to England and met other Separatists in the city of Southampton. In August, along with some others who were not Separatists, they all boarded two ships, the *Speedwell* and the *Mayflower*. They soon discovered that the *Speedwell* was too leaky to make the trip. Both ships landed in the English town of Plymouth, and everyone crammed onto the *Mayflower*.

Slightly more than half of the passengers on the *Mayflower* weren't Separatists. These people hoped to make money in America as farmers, trappers, or merchants. The Separatists called them Strangers. The Separatists and the Strangers who sailed on the *Mayflower* are today known as the Pilgrims. Altogether, there were 102 Pilgrims, including servants. On September 6, the *Mayflower* sailed for North America.

Stranger—a person who traveled on the *Mayflower* from England to Massachusetts but was not a Separatist

Pilgrim—one of the original settlers of Plymouth, either a Separatist or a Stranger

In November, the Pilgrims spotted land. They realized they had reached Cape Cod, not their original goal of northern Virginia. The Pilgrims tried to sail south. As William Bradford later wrote, "*dangerous shoals and roaring [waves]*" forced them back to Cape Cod. With some of their supplies running low, they decided to go ashore. The *Mayflower* anchored at what is now Provincetown. For about one month, the settlers gathered food. They killed ducks and geese and found walnuts. They also discovered corn that had been left behind by Native Americans who lived in the area. The settlers saw Indians several times as they explored.

The Wampanoag

During this time, some of the Pilgrims set out in a small boat to search for the best spot to build their settlement. The location the Pilgrims chose was Plymouth, which John Smith had named Patuxet after the Indian village of the same name. In late December, the *Mayflower* anchored there. The Pilgrims were surprised but pleased to see that fields near the shore had been cleared for farming. Some historians think the Pilgrims may have taken the cleared fields as a sign from God to stay at Plymouth.

The fields had been farmland for some Wampanoag Indians who had once lived in the nearby village of Patuxet. The Wampanoag were part of a larger group of Indians known as the Algonquian. Disease brought to North America by other Europeans had killed all the Indians in the village a few years before.

Life at Sea

The *Mayflower*'s trip across the Atlantic took about two months. The Pilgrims spent as much time on deck as possible. Below deck, the living space was crowded and cramped. Space was so tight that some people had to sleep in a small boat stowed under the top deck.

One crewmember and one passenger became sick and died during the voyage, and three women had babies before the *Mayflower* reached its final stop. William Bradford later wrote that the passengers "*were not a little joyful*" when the trip finally ended.

The Pilgrims quickly began constructing a meeting hall and small huts for families to live in. They slept on board the *Mayflower* while they built their new homes. That winter was a hard one for the Pilgrims. Sickness killed almost half of them, and food supplies ran dangerously low. In the spring, an Abenaki Indian named Samoset appeared. Samoset had learned some English from sailors who came ashore in his homeland to the north, which the English later named Maine. The Indian was now living with the Wampanoag, about 40 miles (64 km) away.

Samoset soon introduced the colonists to Tisquantum (Squanto), a Wampanoag who spoke even more English. Tisquantum had been kidnapped by an Englishman several years before and taken to Spain. He had escaped and lived in England. There, Tisquantum had met Thomas Dermer, a sea captain. Dermer had taken Tisquantum back to North America because the captain had wanted to trade with the Wampanoag.

archaeologist—scientist who studies the past by uncovering items people used in their daily lives

Both Samoset and Tisquantum told the Wampanoag chief, Massasoit, about the Pilgrims. Massasoit ruled a group of tribes that spread over part of present-day Rhode Island and southeastern Massachusetts. Massasoit's people had lived in the area around Patuxet for at least 7,000 years.

Massasoit hoped the Pilgrims would help the Wampanoag if enemy tribes ever attacked. Likewise, the chief and his warriors could aid the Pilgrims if they were attacked. Both the Wampanoag and the Pilgrims saw the value in making friends with each other.

Over the next few months, Tisquantum showed the Pilgrims the best fishing spots and taught them how to plant corn. Bradford wrote in his diary that Tisquantum *"became a special instrument sent of God for [our] good."* The Pilgrims had a plentiful harvest in the fall of 1621. To celebrate, the Pilgrims invited the Wampanoag to join them at a harvest festival that Americans today remember with the Thanksgiving holiday.

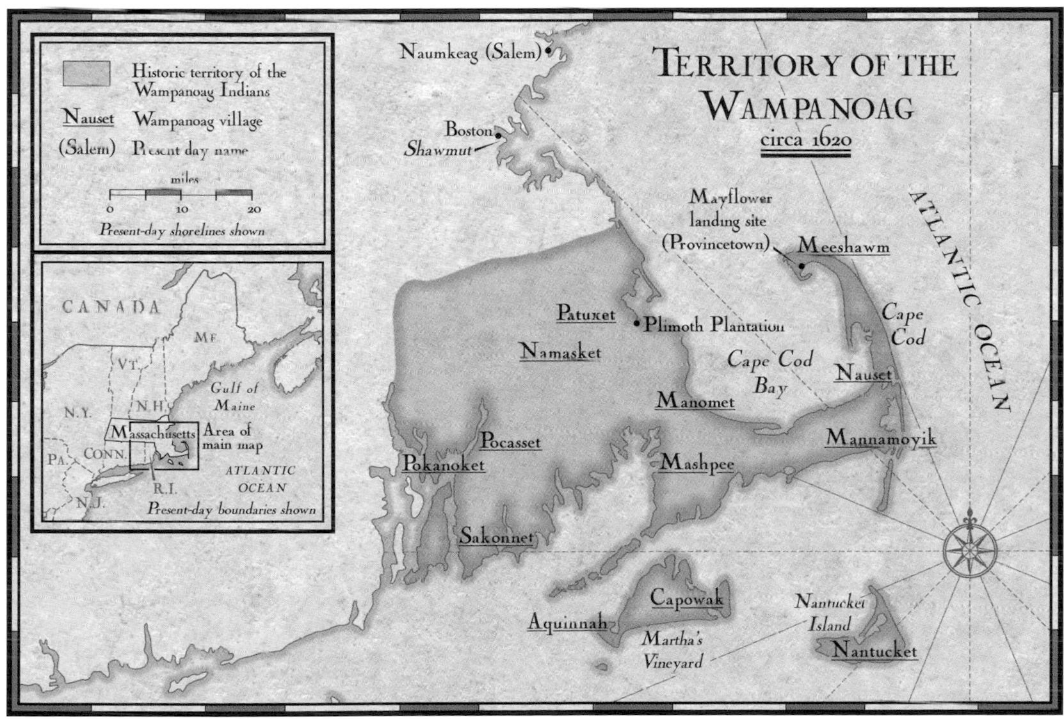

This map shows Wampanoag land at the time of the Pilgrim's arrival in 1620. This area, except for the islands of Martha's Vineyard and Nantucket, became part of the Plymouth Colony. Other Puritans soon settled at Naumkeag and Shawmut, which became part of Massachusetts Bay Colony.

The First Thanksgiving

The celebration of 1621 was not Thanksgiving as the Pilgrims knew it. The day that they called Thanksgiving was not a yearly celebration. Instead, the Pilgrims occasionally set aside one day as a religious holiday that they spent in church, thanking God. Still, the festival the Pilgrims held after their first harvest is now considered the model for the modern Thanksgiving. In a letter to England, Edward Winslow described the event:

> *[William Bradford] sent four men [hunting for fowl], so that we might, after a special manner, rejoice together . . . many of the Indians coming among us [and] for three days we entertained and feasted; and they went out and killed five deer, which they brought to the plantation.*

The Puritans Head for Massachusetts

By 1620, when the Separatists sailed for North America, some English investors had also become interested in New England. These merchants and landowners wanted to make money by sending colonists to Massachusetts. The settlers would fish, raise crops, cut down trees for lumber, and send these resources back to England.

The Dorchester Company sent a group of settlers to Massachusetts in 1625. They founded Naumkeag, named for a nearby Indian village. Some of those who had invested in the Dorchester Company then formed the Massachusetts Bay Company. In 1628, the Massachusetts Bay Company sent about 50 settlers—mostly Puritans—to live in Naumkeag.

In March 1630, almost 1,000 Puritans left England for Massachusetts. They were led by John Winthrop, who was part of the Massachusetts Bay Company. In June, the settlers landed at Naumkeag, recently renamed Salem. Most of the settlers moved on, reaching a region the Indians called Shawmut. In September 1630, Winthrop chose this spot as the capital of the Massachusetts Bay Colony, and the Puritans called it Boston. Winthrop served as the first governor of Massachusetts Bay. The two colonies of Massachusetts—Plymouth and Massachusetts Bay—were now established. ※

John Winthrop, of the Massachusetts Bay Company, led a group of Puritans from England to settle in Salem, Massachusetts.

CHAPTER TWO

Politics in Two Colonies

THE PURITANS AND PILGRIMS *form governments in their Massachusetts colonies.*

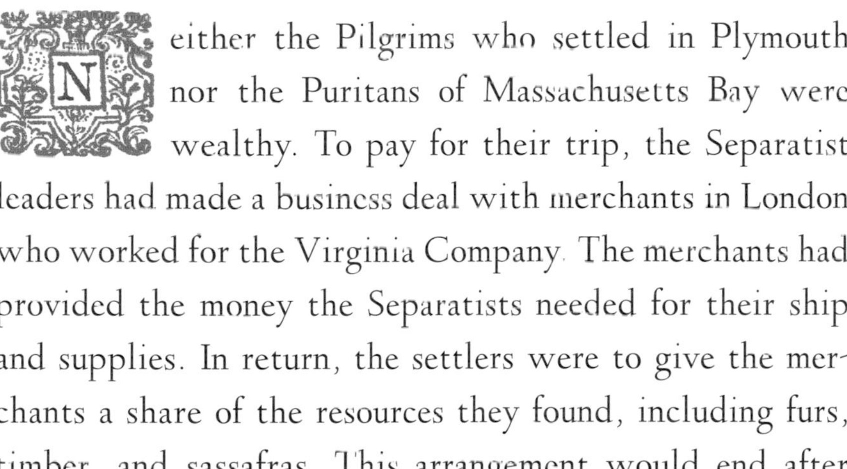

Neither the Pilgrims who settled in Plymouth nor the Puritans of Massachusetts Bay were wealthy. To pay for their trip, the Separatist leaders had made a business deal with merchants in London who worked for the Virginia Company. The merchants had provided the money the Separatists needed for their ship and supplies. In return, the settlers were to give the merchants a share of the resources they found, including furs, timber, and sassafras. This arrangement would end after

OPPOSITE: This 19th-century painting by J.L.G. Ferris shows Stranger and Separatist alike signing the Mayflower Compact, an agreement establishing government and laws among the settlers who arrived on Cape Cod aboard the *Mayflower*.

seven years, and then the settlers could sell their resources wherever they chose.

The contract between the Virginia Company and the Pilgrims assumed that the settlers would land in northern Virginia. When the settlers reached Cape Cod instead, some of the Strangers doubted that the original contract still applied. According to William Bradford, "*When they [the Strangers] came ashore, they would use their own liberty, [do as they pleased] for none had power to command them.*"

The Separatist leaders decided that all the healthy adult males that had come on the *Mayflower*, both Stranger and Separatist, would sign a type of contract called a covenant. Puritans had long used covenants to create congregations. Forty-one people, including some of the servants, signed the Pilgrims' covenant. They agreed to form a government and follow the laws this government created. Now, even though the Pilgrims were beyond the control of the Virginia Company, they would have political order. U.S. historians later named the Pilgrims' covenant the Mayflower Compact.

The men who signed the Mayflower Compact elected John Carver as the first governor of "Plimoth Plantation"—their name for the new colony. Carver died in 1621, and William Bradford took over as governor, a position he held for 30 years. The governor was elected by the colony's freemen—adult males who were not indentured servants. Settlers did not have to be

indentured servant—a person who agreed to work for a period of time, usually five to seven years, in exchange for paid passage to a colony

Separatists to be considered freemen. The freemen also formed the General Court, which passed laws and set taxes.

The original Plymouth settlers were soon joined by new arrivals. By 1623, the colony included a small village with about 20 houses and a fort, surrounded by a large wooden fence. Over time, new towns arose outside the original settlement. The General Court continued to handle political affairs for the colony as a whole. However, local landowners regularly met at town meetings to settle local issues, such as land disputes. Landowners in each town also chose public officials called selectmen, who ran the local government in between the town meetings and also ran the meetings. This form of local government was also common in Massachusetts Bay, but with some important differences.

THE Mayflower Compact

HERE IS PART OF THE COVENANT the Pilgrims signed when they reached Massachusetts:

We, whose names are underwritten . . . do . . . solemnly and mutually, in the presence of God and one another, covenant and combine ourselves together into a civil body politic, for our better ordering and preservation . . . and by virtue hereof do enact, constitute, and frame, such just and equal laws . . . as shall be thought most meet and convenient for the general good of the colony; unto which we promise all due submission and obedience.

THE PURITAN CHARTER

The Massachusetts Bay Colony charter spelled out the basic form of government for the Puritan colony. Members of the Massachusetts Bay Company and freemen were to create a General Court that would meet four times a year. Once a year, the freemen would elect a governor and 18 assistants.

charter—a written document that grants a colony certain rights and privileges, including the right to exist

Less than 20 members of the company actually went to Massachusetts. At first, the members who did go, such as John Winthrop, let all freemen take part in the General Court, whether they were company members or not. However, the members ignored some of the charter's instructions. They let voters choose only the assistants. The assistants then elected the governor. Also, according to the charter, the freemen should have helped make laws, as they did in Plymouth. Instead, Winthrop and the other members said that just the governor and his assistants could make the laws. In 1631, only freemen who were members of the Congregational church could be voting freemen.

Three years later, the General Court asserted its right to be the colony's legislature, or lawmaking body. By this time, the colony's population of freemen was growing, and the lawmakers decided that voters would elect representatives to vote for them in most General Court meetings. Once a year, all freemen would still come to the court to vote for a governor and the governor's assistants.

"TROUBLEMAKERS" IN THE COLONIES

Although most settlers in both colonies had similar Puritan beliefs, some religious and social differences did exist. For example, Roger Williams, a minister, arrived in Boston in 1631. More of a Separatist than a Puritan, he turned down a job at a Boston church and went to Plymouth. His views differed from some of the officials there, however, and he returned to Massachusetts Bay.

Roger Williams was one of the first settlers to publicly challenge the laws fining people who didn't attend church. He was banished from the Massachusetts Bay Colony by Puritan leaders in 1635.

Williams challenged the Puritans' political authority. He opposed a law that fined people who didn't go to church. When religion and government mixed, Williams thought, political issues polluted religion. He wrote, "*The laws of the civil . . . government extend no further than over the body or goods. For over the soul God will not [let] any man to rule, only He himself will rule there.*" Given his beliefs, Williams thought that non-Christians could be good people, another idea that the Puritans rejected.

Finally, in 1635, the Puritans kicked Williams out of the church and banished him from the colony. Williams had earlier bought land in what is now Rhode Island, where he set up a new colony that he called Providence. There, Williams accepted people with a wide range of religious beliefs.

Anne Hutchinson, who arrived in Massachusetts Bay in 1634, was another person who challenged traditional Puritan teachings. At meetings in her home, she expressed religious ideas that went against some official teachings of the church. Hutchinson thought that true Christians were filled with a Holy Spirit sent from God. The spirit guided their actions so they didn't have to follow laws and rules set by humans. Some Puritan leaders saw Hutchinson as a threat to social order. They didn't want people to think that the Puritans had God's permission to ignore laws.

In 1637, Winthrop and other Puritan leaders arrested Hutchinson for denying the authority of the ministers.

Recently, historians have argued that Hutchinson's arrest was part of a larger battle in Massachusetts Bay Colony. Personal conflicts and the desire for political power fueled the debate between Puritans who supported Hutchinson and those who opposed her. At her trial, Hutchinson said laws and rules were *"for those who have not the light which makes plain the pathway."* Hutchinson was banished from Massachusetts Bay. She helped found a new town called Portsmouth. This town later became part of Rhode Island.

The *Mother* COLONY

In addition to Rhode Island, the people of Massachusetts played a role in settling other colonies. During the 1630s, residents from both Plymouth and Massachusetts Bay founded towns along the Connecticut River, about 90 miles (145 km) west of Boston. These towns later united into the colony of Connecticut. During the 1640s, Massachusetts Bay took control of several towns in what is now New Hampshire. Puritans from the Boston area had helped settle those towns. New Hampshire became a separate colony in 1679. Two years earlier, Massachusetts Bay leaders bought the rights to the province of Maine from English investors. Maine remained a province of Massachusetts Bay until 1820.

In 1677, Massachusetts was made up of Plymouth Colony and Massachusetts Bay Colony plus the areas of New Hampshire, Maine, Martha's Vineyard, and Nantucket (brown area on map). The colonies of Connecticut and Rhode Island were originally settled by people from Massachusetts.

Trouble with the Native Americans

Over time, tensions over land divided the Indians and the English. The Native Americans had very different ideas about property and property rights than the Europeans. The Indians accepted goods from the English, believing that they were being paid for permission to use the land. However, the natives believed that they, too, would continue to use the same land. The English, on the other hand, treated land sales just as they did back home in Europe: Once they had purchased a parcel of land, they believed that the Indians no longer had any right to use it. Also, at times, the settlers simply took Indian land without paying for it.

English farming practices also angered the Indians. The settlers cleared large tracts of forest so they could raise corn and farm animals, such as cattle, pigs, and horses. Cutting down the trees destroyed the habitats of the wild animals that the Indians hunted for food. The settlers' farm animals also ran through the Indians' fields, sometimes damaging crops.

New England's first major Indian war erupted in 1636. Puritan leaders in the two Massachusetts colonies and Connecticut blamed the Pequot tribe for the murder of two colonial traders. The Pequot lived in southeastern Connecticut, along Long Island Sound. Massachusetts Bay leaders organized a large army of both settlers and Mohegan

Indian warriors. In July 1636, this force raided Block Island, the home of some Narragansett Indians friendly with the Pequot. The next spring, Connecticut soldiers joined the battle, and the combined Puritan-Mohegan force attacked the main Pequot village in southeastern Connecticut. The battle that followed was one of the bloodiest in colonial American history. The English defeated their enemy in the Pequot War (1636–1637), and for several decades afterward, the Massachusetts colonies grew without worry of Indian attacks.

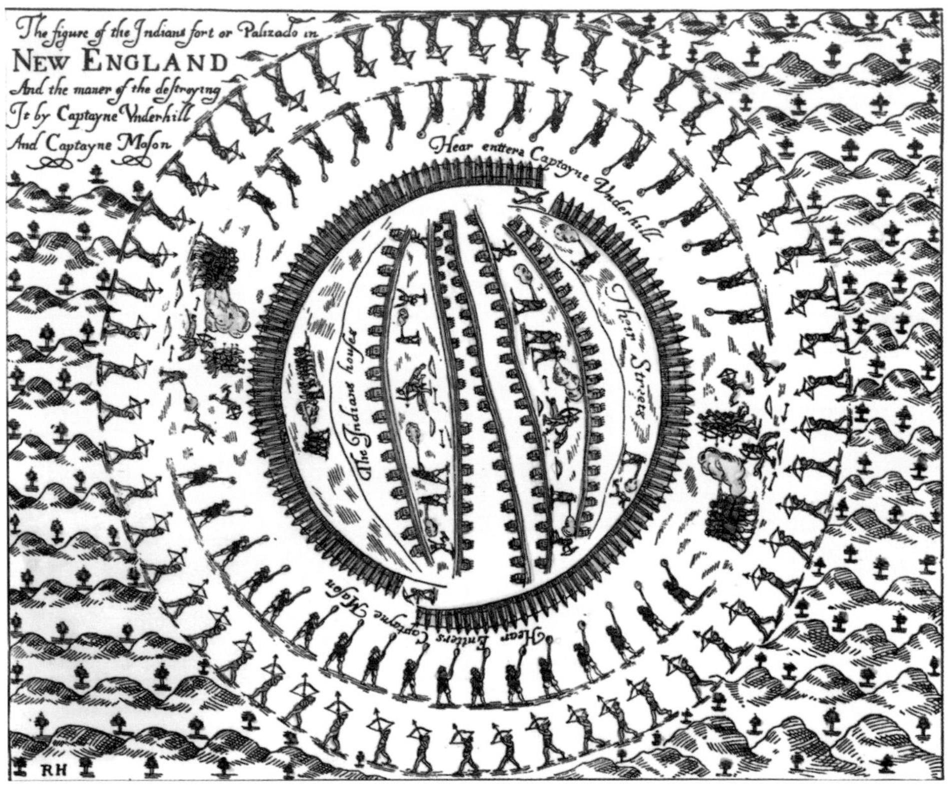

This hand-colored woodcut illustrates the bloody battle between the English and the Pequot tribe in 1637. The Pequot were destroyed and the Massachusetts colonies enjoyed freedom from Indian attacks for many years.

The HORRORS *of* WAR

THE PEQUOT VILLAGE THAT WAS ATTACKED BY Massachusetts and Connecticut Puritans in 1637 was protected by a stockade, a tall, thick wooden fence. After the first attack, the English managed to set fire to the homes, called wigwams, inside the stockade. As the desperate Pequot fled the fast-moving flames, the settlers' Mohegan allies killed them. Hundreds of Pequot who couldn't escape, mostly women and children, died in the fire. William Bradford later described the gruesome scene:

> *It was a fearful sight to see them thus frying in the fire and the streams of blood quenching the same, and horrible was the stink and scent thereof.*

Most Indians rejected Christian teachings, so the Puritans thought their victory was a sign that God approved of Puritan habits and beliefs. For the Pequot, the defeat meant the end of their independence. The English forced about 2,000 survivors to live with Indian tribes they were allied with, including the Mohegan.

CHAPTER THREE

Early Colonial Life

MASSACHUSETTS SETTLERS ADJUST *to daily life in a new land.*

In both the New World and the Old, farming was the most common job during the 17th century. The colonists arrived in Massachusetts with farm tools, seeds, and animals. Clearing and preparing the New England soil was hard work, since many areas were covered with rocks and hills. The soil and climate kept Massachusetts settlers from raising such crops as sugar and tobacco, which could be sold for a profit overseas. The farming conditions also prevented them from

OPPOSITE: Massachusetts colonists brought their farming skills to the New World, but rocky soil conditions and a shorter growing season made growing crops difficult.

raising more than the crops and livestock they needed just to feed themselves. Hunting and fishing helped the settlers complete their diet.

Colonial farmers worked from sunrise to sunset. Each season brought different chores: planting in the spring, tending crops in the summer, harvesting in the fall. Winter gave farmers a chance to fix tools or make new ones and prepare for another year of planting. Even people who had other jobs—blacksmiths, innkeepers, mill owners—had a plot of land that they farmed. Massachusetts resident Edward Johnson wrote that land was so cheap, even *"the poorest person . . . hath a house and land of his own, and bread of his own growing, if not some cattle."*

Crops and Methods

The Indians introduced the settlers to new foods such as pumpkins and other kinds of squash, as well as native fruits, such as blueberries and cranberries. The English also brought seeds with them to raise crops that included wheat, rye, barley, oats, and peas. Farmers planted apple trees and other fruit trees and raised vegetables such as cabbages, carrots, turnips, and beans. The most common farm animals for the first settlers at Plymouth were pigs, chickens, and goats. Over time, oxen, cattle, sheep, and horses were also raised on Massachusetts farms.

By the 1640s, the government in England was controlled by Puritans, both Congregationalists and supporters of a national church. Puritans in England could now freely practice their religion in their homeland. As a result, the number of new arrivals to Massachusetts Bay and Plymouth began to decline. Nevertheless, the population grew as the early settlers had children, who in turn grew up and started their own families. Both colonies expanded as groups of families moved away from the first settlements to start their own communities.

New Ways to Wealth

Since farmers now produced a surplus of food, some Massachusetts settlers turned to other kinds of work. Settlers who had been fishermen and boat builders in England used their skills to create a

During the 1620s and 1630s, bad weather in England led to poor harvests. People faced rising food costs, and if they couldn't afford them or didn't have land to grow food, they starved. For the Puritans, the economy, combined with limits on their religious activities, led them to seek a new home. About 14,000 Puritans headed for New England in what is called the Great Migration of the 1630s. About twice as many more settled in colonies south of New England.

fishing industry. Cod was the main catch, and small fishing fleets sailed out of Gloucester, Marblehead, and other towns along the coast. In Massachusetts Bay, a new law helped the fishing industry grow. People who bought fishing boats and equipment didn't have to pay taxes on them for seven years.

Cod fishing became an important industry as colonists used their skills to become boatbuilders and tax laws favoring fishermen were passed.

The settlers were blessed with plenty of timber to build their boats and ships. The forests of Massachusetts and the rest of New England were filled with cedar, beech, oak, pine, maple, and other trees. Residents of Massachusetts Bay bought forests across the region. Some built sawmills to turn newly cut trees into lumber.

staves—pieces of wood used to make barrels

Wood products from Massachusetts included masts for English sailing ships, wooden shingles, and staves.

Shipbuilding became a key industry for Massachusetts Bay. Most of the boom in shipbuilding came toward the end of the 17th century. Building one ship of 150 tons (136 mt)—slightly larger than the *Mayflower*—took hundreds of workers. Most of the first ships built in Massachusetts were bought by local merchants, but some were also sold in England.

Woodworking was another important industry in early Massachusetts. Skilled woodworkers made tables, chairs, wooden boxes, and barrels. Other artisans included blacksmiths and tailors. A few people also made goods out of metal. In 1646, John Winthrop, Jr. opened the first ironworks in colonial America. This early factory produced raw iron used to make things such as kettles, tools, and nails.

Starting in the 1640s, Massachusetts merchants used locally built ships to carry cod and wood products overseas. The ships brought back goods such as wine, olive oil, and sugar. Massachusetts merchants also became part of the slave trade. Their ships carried slaves from Africa to the islands of the West Indies. From there, the ships brought sugar and molasses to New England. This trade between Africa, the West Indies, and North America was sometimes called the triangle trade because the route ships sailed resembled a triangle.

The Diary of THOMAS SHEPARD

MANY PURITANS KEPT DIARIES TO RECORD THEIR THOUGHTS on God's role in their lives. Thomas Shepard was a minister in Boston who wrote a diary for his son. A selection from this diary shows the Puritans' belief that God played an active role in their lives:

[God] took away my most dear, precious, meek, and loving wife. . . . This affliction was very heavy to me, for in it the Lord seemed to withdraw His tender care for me and mine, which He graciously [showed] by my dear wife; also refused to hear prayer when I did think He would have harkened and let me see His beauty in the land of the living . . . but I am the Lord's and He may do with me what He will.

RELIGION IN DAILY LIFE

The Massachusetts Bay colonists devoted a great deal of time to their farming and commerce, yet they always kept their religious faith central to their daily concerns. They saw God's influence in everything that happened to them, good or bad, and believed they must prepare themselves in the hope that they would go to heaven. This meant studying the Bible, praying, going to church services, and following God's word.

Religion shaped the laws of Massachusetts Bay and Plymouth. Ministers were not allowed to serve in the government, but most elected officials were devout Puritans. Not surprisingly, many laws in Massachusetts Bay were based on the Bible. The commandment to "keep holy the Sabbath" meant people could do very few things except attend church services on Sundays. A 1658 law in Massachusetts Bay called for fining *"all youths and maids above 14 years old, and all elder persons . . . for playing, uncivil walking, drinking, traveling from town to town, going on ship-board, sporting, or any way misspending that precious time."*

Even in harsh weather, Pilgrims traveled to church to obey the laws of God. Many believed that the success or failure of their colony depended upon the strength of their faith and devotion.

Family Life

Religion also shaped the Puritans' beliefs about the relationships between people. The Puritans said that God gave men the right to rule over their wives and children. Most women married, and they were expected to obey their husbands. Anything that a single woman owned became her husband's property when she married. A wife could not own property as long as her husband was alive. Women could not vote or serve in government. (In the United States, women would not win the right to vote until 1920.)

Still, women in colonial Massachusetts had some rights and protection. Husbands could be arrested for beating their wives, and women had the right to make some legal agreements. In Plymouth, several widows who wanted to remarry signed contracts with their future husbands about the property each woman brought to the

APPRENTICES

APPRENTICING CHILDREN WAS an old English practice. Parents arranged for their child to live with a skilled master artisan for seven years. Besides providing food and shelter, the master taught the apprentice the skills of the craft. In return for this education, the apprentices helped the masters in their work. Most apprentices were boys between the ages of 10 and 14 who would learn skills such as shoemaking or carpentry. Some girls also became apprentices, learning skills such as weaving and sewing.

marriage. The agreements spelled out what would happen to each woman's property after she died.

A typical 17th-century woman in Massachusetts had two main duties: raising the children and taking care of the house. Children learned the basics of reading either at home from their parents or at school. Girls learned household chores such as sewing and cooking. Boys learned farming, in addition to whatever other skills their fathers could teach them, such as carpentry. Some children were sent to live as apprentices with neighbors so they could learn a skill.

Education

Puritans believed that all children should receive at least a basic education. In 1642, Massachusetts Bay passed a law requiring fathers and masters to teach their children and apprentices how to read. A 1647 law required towns to educate children, since the General Court believed that *"one chief project of that old deluder, Satan, [was] to keep men from the knowledge of the [Bible]."* A town with 50 households had to hire someone to teach reading and writing, and towns with 100 households or more had to build a grammar school. Some towns had already opened schools before this law was passed.

In 1636, the General Court of Massachusetts Bay created what later became Harvard College. Only boys attended college at this time, and they usually entered when they were 14 or 15 years old. Students who went to

CHRISTMAS *in* Massachusetts

ONE SPECIAL DAY THE PURITANS didn't observe was Christmas. Since the Bible doesn't say when Jesus Christ was born, Puritans rejected December 25 as his birth date. Non-Puritans in Massachusetts, however, did celebrate the holiday as they had in England, with public games, large meals, dancing, and drinking.

In 1659, the Massachusetts Bay General Court made it a crime to celebrate Christmas in public, calling it a "*great dishonor of God and offense of others.*" The law was later repealed, but the Puritans still looked down on people who celebrated December 25 as the birth of Jesus.

Harvard or a college in England were expected to be able to read and write in Latin as well as English. At Harvard, students continued to study Latin as well as math, history, logic, astronomy, and ethics—the study of good and bad behavior.

RECREATION AND CULTURE

Ethical behavior was always the goal in every part of Puritan life. The colonists believed that such activities as dancing or playing cards took time away from studying the Bible, which taught them to live according to God's rules. Still, the Puritans didn't forbid all pleasures. People gathered to celebrate weddings and other special occasions. They played some games, as well. Several decades after the founding of Massachusetts Bay, John Dunton wrote about people playing an early form of what Americans now call soccer. The English called the game football, as they still do today. Dunton described how players *"played with their bare feet, which I thought was very odd."*

Residents of colonial Massachusetts also enjoyed a form of outdoor bowling. During the 1990s, the state of Massachusetts began a massive building project in Boston called the Big Dig. The work uncovered many everyday items from colonial times. One of the finds was an oak bowling ball shaped like a wheel, made between 1660 and 1715.

Although the Puritans focused their lives around the Bible, they also read ancient works by Greek and Latin writers. Some found time to write poetry. Anne Bradstreet is the best-known poet of 17th-century Massachusetts. Her most famous poem is "To My Dear and Loving Husband." For centuries, many Americans thought the Puritans were serious people who lacked affection for each other. Modern historians like the Bradstreet poem because it helps destroy that myth. Bradstreet wrote, *"I prize thy love more than whole mines of gold, or all the riches that the East dost hold."*

Puritan clothing was usually made of simple black cloth and had few, if any, decorations. Puritans believed in modesty before God, and anything fancy indicated attention to something other than worship.

CHAPTER FOUR

Difficult Decades

AN INDIAN WAR AND TROUBLE *in England shape events in Massachusetts.*

s the 1660s began, the number of non-Puritans in Massachusetts continued to increase, as it had since the end of the Great Migration. More of the new settlers who came to Massachusetts were looking for land or business opportunities rather than religious freedom. Ministers and government officials worried that the newcomers would weaken Puritan beliefs.

Changes in England also affected the North American colonies. During the 1640s, forces loyal to King Charles I

OPPOSITE: This woodcut illustrates the execution of King Charles I outside Whitehall Palace in London, England, in 1649.

battled Puritans and others in Parliament—England's law-making body—who opposed his rule. Under Charles I, the government had arrested some ministers who had insisted on teaching Puritan beliefs. The Puritans were angry with this effort to limit their religious freedom. Charles I had also tried to limit Parliament's power.

The king's Puritan enemies forced him off the throne and executed him in 1649. For a time, the Puritan law-maker Oliver Cromwell led the English government. By the time he died in 1658, England had faced years of civil and foreign wars. The people wanted a king again to help restore order. At Parliament's request, Charles II, the son of Charles I, took over as king in 1660.

During these difficult times, England's rulers didn't pay much attention to their North American colonies. That situation changed after Charles II came to power. Parliament soon passed laws called the Navigation Acts. These laws applied to all the Colonies. One of the laws said that some colonial goods, such as sugar, tobacco, and certain woods, had to be shipped to England before they could be sold in other countries. The Colonies couldn't trade directly with foreign nations, and foreign ships couldn't stop at American ports. Massachusetts merchants and shipbuilders chose to ignore the laws that hurt their businesses and began to smuggle goods.

smuggle—to bring goods into a country illegally

Some English officials began to complain about the American colonies disobeying their charters and the Navigation Acts. In 1664, England sent commissioners to look into these charges. In Massachusetts, the commissioners discovered that the colonists were indeed breaking the law. Parliament might have placed the Colonies under tighter control, but the plague swept through England in 1665, and a terrible fire destroyed most of London the next year. As a result, Massachusetts Bay and Plymouth escaped any real punishment—for a time.

commissioner—a government official who focuses on a specific issue

King Philip's War

Relations with England were not the colonists' only concern. Trouble was brewing with the Wampanoag Indians. The settlers and Indians remained friendly until Massasoit died, around 1661. The Puritans had actively tried to convert the Wampanoag to Christianity. Some tribal leaders feared that the Wampanoag's culture was under attack. If more Indians became Christians, then the traditional religious beliefs would die out. The English were also buying more Wampanoag land. As the settlers cleared the land, they destroyed the Indians' hunting grounds and farmland.

King Philip, son of Massasoit, became Chief of the Wampanoag when his father died.

Praying Towns

Starting in the 1640s, the Puritans of Massachusetts Bay began to teach Christianity to Native Americans. The Reverend John Eliot led this effort. He believed that Christian Indians should settle in permanent towns, away from tribal members who rejected Christianity. In 1651, he founded Natick as the first "praying town"—a separate village for converted Indians. In these towns, the "praying Indians" built meetinghouses and schools and formed their own government. By 1675, about 1,100 Indians lived in these villages across Massachusetts.

By 1671, Massasoit's son Metacom was the Wampanoag sachem, or chief. The settlers called him King Philip. Metacom believed that his people might have to fight to keep their old ways of life. The sachem asked other Indian tribes to become his allies and prepare for war.

In the spring of 1675, the English accused three Wampanoag of killing a Christian Indian. They were found guilty and put to death for their crime. Angered by this, Metacom's warriors raided the colonial town of Swansea, Massachusetts, and one Indian was killed there. The Wampanoag then came back and killed several settlers. A conflict called King Philip's War (1675–1676) was underway.

In the first few months of the war, the Indians terrorized colonists in Massachusetts Bay, Plymouth, Connecticut, and Rhode Island. In 1676, the settlers recruited the Mohegan and their Native American allies for help, as well as Christian Indians in the praying towns. With their larger force, the settlers tracked down Metacom and killed him, ending the bloodiest Indian war in New England's history. Many of the defeated Indians were forced to move west of the Connecticut River. Others were forced into slavery and sold in the West Indies.

King Philip's War ended when Puritans and their Mohegan allies attacked Metacom's fort, killing the Indian leader and many of the Wampanoag tribe.

PROFILE

Mary Rowlandson

Mary Rowlandson was living in Lancaster, Massachusetts, with a husband and children when King Philip's War began. In the winter of 1676, she and some relatives were captured by the Wampanoag or some of their allies and held for almost three months. Rowlandson later wrote about her experience.

. . . we traveled about half a day or little more, and came to a desolate place in the wilderness . . . we came about the middle of the afternoon to this place, cold and wet, and snowy, and hungry, and weary, and no refreshing for man but the cold ground to sit on, and our poor Indian [food]. . . . My head was light and dizzy (either through hunger or hard lodging, or trouble or all together), my knees feeble, my body raw by sitting double night and day, that I cannot express to man the affliction that lay upon my spirit.

A Colony of the King

As King Philip's War was raging, England once again sent someone to investigate the New England colonies. Edward Randolph arrived in Boston in 1676. He was appalled at how many colonists ignored English laws, especially regarding trade. John Leverett, governor of Massachusetts Bay, defended the colonists. He said, "*The king can in reason do no less than let us enjoy our liberties and trade, for we have made this large plantation . . . without any contribution from the crown.*" King Charles II disagreed, and he asked Randolph to collect duties owed the crown.

duty—a tax placed on goods brought into a country

Massachusetts Bay still let only full members of the Congregational Church vote in elections, and only Puritans could worship freely in public. These restrictions limited the rights of English settlers who belonged to the Anglican Church or other Protestant religions. Both the colony's religious laws and its trading practices angered Charles. In 1684, he took back the charter that gave Massachusetts Bay its legal right to exist. Massachusetts Bay became a royal colony and from then on, the king had direct control. The king, not the colonists, would choose the governor. The governor had the power to veto, or reject, laws passed in the General Court and choose many government officials.

Charles died in 1685. His brother, James II, became the new king. James II united Massachusetts Bay, Plymouth, the Province of Maine, and New Hampshire into one unit called the Dominion of New England. (Connecticut, Rhode Island, New York, and New Jersey were added later.) A governor and council, chosen by James II, ruled these united colonies.

The first governor of New England was Sir Edmund Andros. Based in Boston, Andros quickly made drastic changes in government. He planned to take control of lands from current local owners and give it to the king. The new governor also ordered that town meetings could be held only once a year. Andros brought along troops to Massachusetts. People in Massachusetts were forced to pay higher taxes to support the soldiers and to pay Andros's salary.

By 1688, England was going through its own political change. Parliament was controlled by Protestants. James II was a Roman Catholic, and he broke the law by giving Catholics important positions in the government. This greatly angered English Protestants, but they soon found an ally in William of Orange. This Dutch Protestant prince was married to Princess Mary, the Protestant daughter of James II. (Mary had decided to follow her mother's Protestant faith rather than her father's Catholicism.) In November 1688, William landed in England with an army. As it marched on London, James II fled the country. Parliament made William and Mary the king and queen. It also declared that no future monarch could disobey Parliament. The English called these events their "Glorious Revolution," because they had reformed their government without spilling a drop of blood.

The Glorious Revolution—the 1688 bloodless revolution in which English Protestants ousted Catholic King James II and made William and Mary King and Queen of England

A New Charter

The Glorious Revolution gave Massachusetts a welcome chance to get rid of the dreaded Andros. Early in 1689, the residents began to hear rumors from England that James II was no longer king, and they acted quickly against Andros. In Boston, several thousand members of local militia prepared to arrest Andros and some of his aides. Local leaders issued a statement telling Andros that *"for your own safety, we judge it necessary that you forthwith surrender, and deliver up the government and fortifications."* Rather than risk bloodshed, Andros agreed.

militia—a group of citizen-soldiers

The Dominion of New England soon broke up into the separate colonies that had existed before Andros's arrival. Massachusetts Bay and Plymouth ran their governments as they had since each was founded. In the meantime, the colonists waited for the new king to take action.

In 1691, William combined Plymouth and Massachusetts Bay into one colony called Massachusetts. Maine and the islands of Nantucket and Martha's Vineyard were included, as well. William then made Massachusetts a royal colony. He also changed the law so that any freeman could vote, and all Protestants could worship as they chose. For decades, however, local Puritan leaders still kept non-Puritans from openly practicing their faith. Massachusetts would be governed under the royal charter of 1691 for more than 80 years, until the American Revolution (1775–1783).

TORMENT IN SALEM

ANN PUTNAM WAS ONE OF the first girls in Salem who was supposedly afflicted, or affected, by witchcraft. She told officials that if one accused witch *"did but look upon me she would strike me down or almost choke me also . . . I saw Miss Bradbury most grievously afflict and torment Mary Walcott."* In June 1692, the first of several witch trials began. The afflicted girls sometimes shrieked and moaned in court, claiming that the witches were tormenting them again. The judges believed the word of Putnam and other accusers, even though the supposed witches claimed they were innocent.

WITCHES IN SALEM?

In Salem Village in 1692, a group of young girls began to act strangely. They bent their arms in unnatural ways, and odd pinch marks appeared on their skin. The girls accused several local women of putting them under a spell. Within a few months, other women, men, and children were accused of witchcraft.

Massachusetts law said that a person found guilty of being a witch was to be executed. In Salem and surrounding towns, the jails quickly filled with accused witches. Any person who defended the innocence of a supposed witch risked being accused, as well.

By the end of September, 19 people had been executed for witchcraft. Another person had been crushed under a pile of stones because he had refused to testify at a trial. By now, however, some important ministers and political leaders in Boston thought the hunt for witches had gone too far. It seemed impossible that one small area of Massachusetts could produce so many witches. Governor William Phips finally stepped in. He freed many accused witches, and after the last trial in January 1693, he released from jail everyone who been found guilty of witchcraft.

Some historians believe that a chemical in the air caused the afflicted girls in Salem to act strangely. This chemical might have come from a fungus that forms on rye, which the colonists grew. Others note that Salem was divided in 1692. Political and economic tensions between neighbors led to disagreements. People angry with their neighbors might have accused them of witchcraft or been more likely to believe accusations made by others.

This painting illustrates the ordeal many who were accused of witchcraft were forced to endure.

The Salem trials led to the greatest number of executions in a witch scare in American history. The growing belief that innocent people had been wrongly punished prevented future witch hunts in Massachusetts and the rest of New England.

CHAPTER FIVE

Servants and Slaves in Massachusetts

FARMS AND BUSINESSES *rely on slaves and servants to get many things done.*

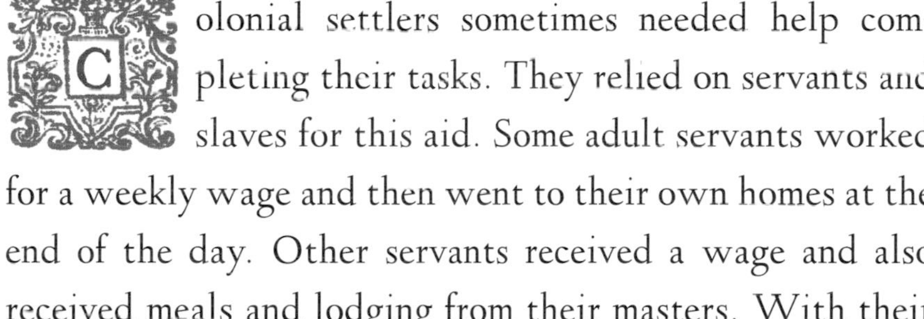

Colonial settlers sometimes needed help completing their tasks. They relied on servants and slaves for this aid. Some adult servants worked for a weekly wage and then went to their own homes at the end of the day. Other servants received a wage and also received meals and lodging from their masters. With their money, most servants hoped to buy land or start a business.

OPPOSITE: Colonial artisans work with various tools of their trades in a field outside the city of Boston.

Servants usually signed a contract called an indenture. Many indentured servants signed contracts in England before coming to Massachusetts. By agreeing to work for a master, the servants earned their voyage to America.

In Massachusetts Bay, the law said that indentured servants who "*have served . . . faithfully to the benefit of their masters seven years shall not be sent away empty.*" Masters had to give tools, clothing, or land to servants when their contracts ended. Indentured servants in Plymouth received similar payments when their contracts ended.

Servant Life

Masters were in charge of servants' lives, and servants were expected to obey their masters. However, masters could not command their servants to break the law.

Some masters were determined to work their servants as hard as possible. Lazy or disobedient servants were punished. Brutal masters would sometimes whip or beat servants. One 13-year-old servant in Plymouth was found dead, his skin "*blackish and blue*" and "*all his back [covered] with [welts] given him by his master.*" The master was later found guilty of manslaughter and had all his property taken away.

Not all masters showed this kind of cruelty. Masters were expected to take good care of their servants, and most did. Servants who completed their indentures might choose to stay with a kind master. If the servants were really lucky, their masters might leave them money in their wills. One Plymouth master gave everything he owned to his servant. The master called him *"my well-beloved friend . . . whom I have brought up from his childhood."*

Servants—and slaves—sometimes ran away from their masters. Some servants just wanted a break from their hard work, and they soon returned. Others ran away for good. In 1648, Massachusetts Bay passed a law designed to catch runaways. The law said public officials could recruit local men *"at the public charge to pursue such persons [runaways] by land or sea and bring them back by force of arms."*

Women servants usually worked as maids in wealthy colonists' homes. The common uniform included a dress called a sacque, an apron, and clogs.

SLAVERY IN COLONIAL TIMES

When Europeans first came to the New World, they enslaved the Native Americans they defeated in battle. Soon, however, the settlers started bringing Africans to the Americas, because they needed more workers for their farms and plantations. Many of these slaves were taken violently from their homes by slave traders—usually other Africans. The slaves

plantation—a large, self-sufficient farm

were marched to ports where they were sold to European slave traders. Then they began a long, frightening journey across the Atlantic Ocean. From 1450 to 1850, the main years of the Atlantic slave trade, more than one million Africans, or 10 percent of those who made the voyage, died during these ocean journeys.

An illustration of English slave traders forcing Africans aboard a skiff that will take them to a slave ship ready to cross the Atlantic Ocean to the New World.

In Massachusetts Bay, the General Court passed its first law on slavery in 1641. The law only allowed slaves who were *"lawful captives, taken in just wars, and such strangers as willingly sell themselves or are sold to us."* Indians were the first slaves in Massachusetts. Most Indian slaves were sold to slave owners in the West Indies, since captive Indians who worked on local farms in Massachusetts could count on nearby Indians to help them escape. The first African slaves reached Massachusetts Bay in 1638. By the end of the 17th century, most slaves in Massachusetts were Africans. Many Massachusetts merchants made profits from the slave trade.

Valuable Property

When the word "servant" appears in colonial writings, it sometimes presents problems for modern historians. "Servant" could refer to a person who had signed an indenture or a person who worked for a salary. Some apprentices were also called servants in written documents.

Colonists would also use the word "servant" to describe a slave. As time went on, African Americans were more likely than Indians to be slaves in Massachusetts. Historians examining life in 17th-century Plymouth found that a master's will often revealed whether a so-called servant was really a slave. If the master said a servant was worth a certain amount of money, the servant was probably a slave. Slaves were considered valuable property and could be bought and sold like any other items.

Africans in Massachusetts

The number of African slaves in Massachusetts remained low through the 17th century. By 1700, the colony had only 500 slaves out of a total population of about 56,000. A little more than 50 years later, Massachusetts had 2,700 adult Africans out of a population of just under 250,000. Although a small number of these blacks were free, most Africans in the colony were slaves. The greatest number lived in Boston and nearby towns along the coast. Only about 10 percent of Massachusetts residents had both the money and the need to own slaves. The average Massachusetts slave owner had fewer than five slaves.

At first, most Massachusetts slaves came from the West Indies. By the 18th century, more came directly from Africa. African slaves, like white servants, were usually considered part of the family, and they ate and lived with their master's family. Masters were expected to educate young slaves, just as they did servants, and make sure slaves were fed and clothed. Yet slaves lacked the basic freedom to do what they wanted when they wanted, more so than indentured servants. Laws also restricted slaves' lives—they were forbidden to marry whites, carry weapons, or sell liquor.

On farms, slaves helped raise crops and livestock. Female slaves often worked inside the house. In 1739, one master wanted to sell a female slave who *"can do all sorts of household work as washing, baking, brewing and can sew very well.*" Some male slaves held skilled jobs. As early as 1661, an African was working with a cooper. African slaves also served as carpenters, blacksmiths, printers, shoemakers, and tailors. Some went to sea as sailors, cooks, or fishermen.

cooper—a person who makes barrels

Africans in Massachusetts tried to keep some of their old culture and religious beliefs and pass them along to their American-born children. For example, African slaves made musical instruments like the ones they knew in Africa. These included fiddles with three strings, banjos, and drums. Some fiddlers would play for other slaves and for whites. ※

A PLEA FOR FREEDOM

On behalf of their fellow slaves in the Massachusetts colony, Peter Estes, Sambo Freeman, Felix Nolbrook, and Chester Joie signed the following letter on April 20, 1773.

The efforts made by the legislative of this province in their last sessions to free themselves from slavery, gave us, who are in that deplorable state, a high degree of satisfaction. We expect great things from men who have made such a noble stand . . . and hope Sir, that you will have . . . civil and religious liberty, in view in your next session. . . .

A New Century

ENGLAND'S WARS WITH FRANCE *come to Massachusetts.*

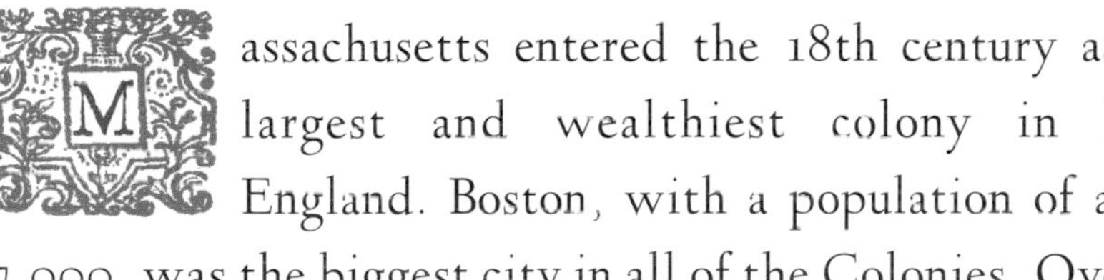

Massachusetts entered the 18th century as the largest and wealthiest colony in New England. Boston, with a population of about 7,000, was the biggest city in all of the Colonies. Overall, the colony did not produce the great wealth that the southern colonies did, thanks to their plantations. If Massachusetts did not have great riches, however, it lacked great poverty. In many areas, land was still plentiful, and most people could find work.

Although now under the king's direct control, Massachusetts enjoyed greater freedom than other royal

OPPOSITE: On February 29, 1704, French and Indian troops attacked the town of Deerfield, Massachusetts, killing and capturing hundreds of settlers in what became known as the Deerfield Massacre.

colonies did. Under the charter of 1691, the members of the General Court chose the governor's advisers, though the governor had final approval. (In other royal colonies, the king chose the governor's advisers.) The advisers served as one half of the General Court. The other half was the House of Representatives. Freemen in Massachusetts elected the members of this assembly, which passed the colony's laws. These laws could be reviewed by the governor's advisers.

The House of Representatives had the sole power to collect taxes and decide how that money was spent. The governor had important powers, as well. He could call the General Court into session when he chose and end the session if he disapproved of what the lawmakers did. The governor also had the power to appoint all judges, and he usually chose men who shared his political views.

Part of an Empire

Massachusetts and the other American colonies were part of the much larger English colonial empire. England and its European rivals, especially France and Spain, competed for influence around the world. When England waged war with these nations, the fighting often spilled over into North America. In New England, France posed the biggest threat to English interests because it controlled New France, in what is now Canada. Together, French and

Indian forces terrorized Maine and other parts of Massachusetts.

In February 1704, the French and Indians attacked Deerfield, in western Massachusetts. About 50 settlers were killed and 100 or so more were taken to New France. One of these captives was John Williams, a minister. He described the raid in his book, *The Redeemed Captive Returning to Zion*. He wrote that "*not long before break of day, the enemy came in like a flood upon us. . . . They came to my house . . . and by their violent endeavors to break open doors and windows, with axes and hatchets, awaked me out of sleep.*" Williams spent more than two years in New France before returning to Massachusetts.

Battling France

The Deerfield raid was part of a war between Great Britain and France called Queen Anne's War (1702–1713). During this war, Massachusetts soldiers fought several times in New France. At the end of the war, Great Britain won control of Nova Scotia, a region of New France on the Atlantic Ocean.

In 1743, France and Great Britain fought again, in a conflict called King George's War (1743–1748). The French still had a presence just off Nova Scotia, on Cape Breton Island. Their massive fort there, called Louisbourg, had stone walls that were 30 feet (9 m) high, and more than

100 cannon defended the site. The French commander at Louisbourg ordered his ships to capture New England's merchant vessels.

Massachusetts governor William Shirley soon organized a militia of about 4,500 soldiers from across New England—more than 3,000 from Massachusetts alone—commanded by William Pepperell. In April 1745, the soldiers sailed from Boston for Nova Scotia. British warships provided extra firepower for the invading New Englanders.

Pepperell's men first took control of a battery of French cannon just outside the fort. One resident of Louisbourg later wrote that the New Englanders *"saluted us with our own cannon, and made a terrific fire, smashing everything within range."*

battery—a group of large weapons in one location

PEPPERELL'S *REPORT*

BORN IN MAINE, WILLIAM PEPPERELL SPENT MANY YEARS in Boston as a representative at the General Court. He also served as a judge there. Pepperell sent Governor Shirley a report on the battle at Louisbourg. He wrote, *"Never was a place more mauled with cannon and shells. Neither have I read in history of any troops behaving with greater courage. We gave them about nine thousand cannonballs and six hundred bombs."*

Pepperell's troops then opened fire on the fort itself. At sea, the British fleet prevented the French from landing more troops, and in June, the French surrendered. However, in the peace treaty that ended the war, Great Britain and France agreed to give back lands they had seized from each other, and Louisbourg returned to French control.

William Pepperell sits astride his horse as he surveys the battle scene at Louisbourg. The English were victorious over the French in the bloody battle.

More Trouble with the French and Indians

Massachusetts and other English colonies in America still faced a threat from Indians and their French allies. Both the French and the English sought control of fur-rich lands in Ohio Country. The threat turned to real warfare in 1754. A young Virginia officer named George Washington fought French and Indian forces near the Ohio River. These were the first battles of what Americans later called the French and Indian War (1754–1763). Other fighting between the British and the French at this time took place in Europe and the West Indies.

In 1755, Great Britain sent troops to America to protect settlers along the northern and western frontier that bordered French territory. Governor Shirley sent several thousand Massachusetts troops into battle. They fought in Nova Scotia, where the French were trying to build new forts. Massachusetts soldiers also fought near Lake George, in upstate New York, where the French had already built a fort.

frontier—wilderness that borders a settled area

In 1758, the British government asked Massachusetts to recruit 7,000 soldiers. Thousands more joined the war in the next two years. The French and their Indian allies battled the British and their Native American supporters in many of the 13 Colonies and what would become Canada.

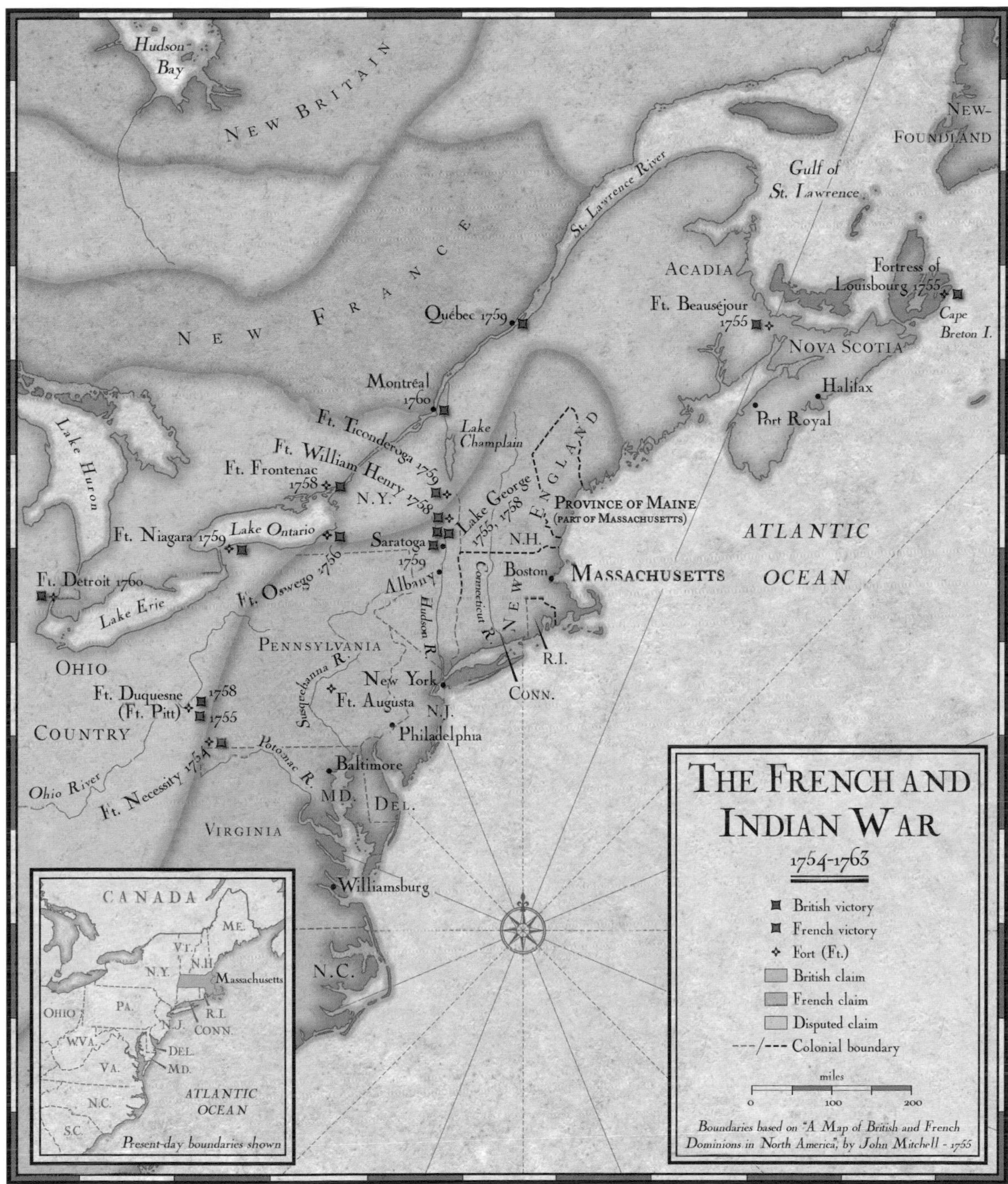

Victory in the French and Indian War gave Britain control of all lands claimed by France in what is now Canada and the United States. The outcome ended raids on Massachusetts territory but created serious problems over British taxes and trade restrictions.

In 1759, the British won a major victory outside Quebec City, and another the next year in Montreal. The war was mostly over in North America after that, although fighting continued in other parts of the world.

The wars of the mid-18th century affected Massachusetts's relations with Great Britain. British naval captains came to Boston and forced civilian sailors to serve on British warships. This practice was called impressment, and the colonists hated it. Merchants lost the sailors they needed to run their ships, and the impressed sailors were treated almost as badly as slaves.

Massachusetts colonists also disliked British attempts to control colonial trade. The British wanted most trade to go through its ports. Merchants continued to smuggle goods from the West Indies and Europe. British officials used legal documents called writs of assistance to clamp down on smugglers. The writs allowed British officials to board ships and enter shops and homes to search for smuggled goods.

On the Frontier

During the French & Indian War, many Massachusetts soldiers found it hard to travel in the remote regions of western Massachusetts and New York. One soldier wrote, "*We had no other road than marked trees to direct our course, no bridges on which to cross the streams; some of which we waded; others we passed on trees felled by our men; and for five successive nights we lay on the ground.*"

As the French and Indian War was ending in North America, the British wanted to use the writs more often. The government had spent huge amounts of money during the war. Now it wanted to collect all the duties it was owed. Boston merchants went to court to stop the British from using new writs of assistance. James Otis and Oxenbridge Thatcher were the merchants' lawyers. In February 1761, they called the writs *"most destructive of English liberty and the fundamental principles of law."* Otis and Thatcher lost their case, but their arguments about liberty and the rights of Americans became more common in the years before the American Revolution. ※

A Growing Colony

THE COLONY SEES INCREASED WEALTH, *changing roles for women, and new religious concerns.*

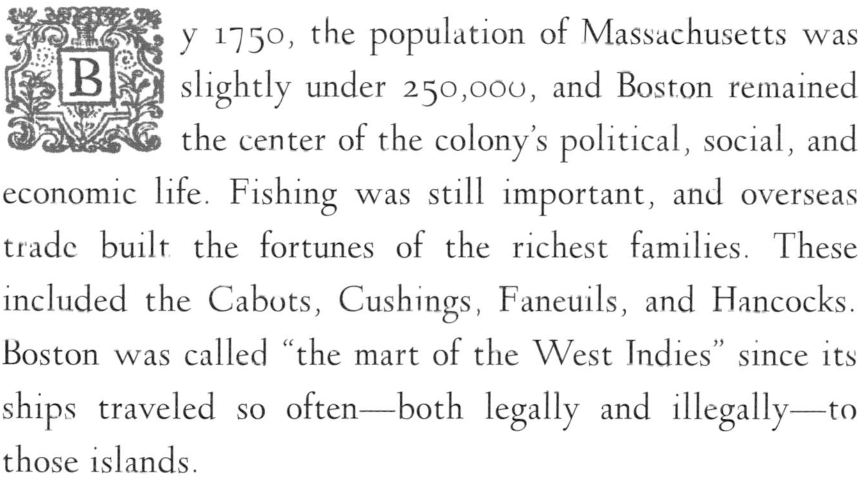

By 1750, the population of Massachusetts was slightly under 250,000, and Boston remained the center of the colony's political, social, and economic life. Fishing was still important, and overseas trade built the fortunes of the richest families. These included the Cabots, Cushings, Faneuils, and Hancocks. Boston was called "the mart of the West Indies" since its ships traveled so often—both legally and illegally—to those islands.

OPPOSITE: Faneuil Hall, which still stands as a center of commerce in Boston today, was built by the Faneuils, one of the richest families living in 18th-century Massachusetts.

This engraving of the city of Boston, by Paul Revere, appeared in the first issue of *Royal American Magazine* in January 1774.

Some of the colony's most successful men started with very little. For example, Thomas Hancock arrived in Boston in 1717 where he became a bookbinder, someone who assembled bound books. A few years later, Hancock opened a bookstore and then became part owner of a paper factory. As his wealth grew, Hancock looked for new business opportunities. He bought whale oil from Nantucket whalers and sold it in England. Whale oil was used to fuel lamps. With the money he made, Hancock bought items to sell in his store. Eventually, he bought his own ships to carry his goods.

Thanks to merchants like Hancock, a wide variety of goods appeared in Boston shops. They included fine cloth and clothing, china, tools, and kitchen utensils. As the supply of manufactured items from England and other colonies rose, their prices fell. This meant more people could afford to buy goods than in the past.

Early industries such as shipbuilding and lumbering continued to grow. Mills of all kinds used waterpower to turn natural resources into finished products. Making paper was a colonial industry in Massachusetts—the colony and neighboring lands in New Hampshire had plenty of forests and rivers that could power the mills that turned trees into paper. Yet many of the items needed for daily life came from individual artisans. Carpenters made furniture, metalsmiths created tools and silverware, and coopers made barrels. More expensive items, such as fine cloth or fancy dishes, came from Great Britain.

Support for Smuggling

Some overseas traders continued to make their money through smuggling. In 1743, a British official in Massachusetts reported about smuggling:

. . . the persons concerned in this trade [smuggling] are many, some of them of the greatest fortunes in this country, and who have made great gains by it; and, having all felt the sweets of it, they begin to [promote] it and justify it . . . and having persuaded themselves that their trade ought not to be bound by the laws of Great Britain, they labor . . . to poison the minds of all the inhabitants of the province.

On the Farm

Despite the rise of wealthy merchants, most people still earned their living as farmers. Through much of the 18th century, Massachusetts farms couldn't always produce enough food to feed the whole colony. Residents had to buy some crops from other colonies or from Great Britain. Raising livestock was more successful. Farmers raised sheep for wool and meat that were then sold in other colonies. Cows produced milk and meat both for local families and for markets outside Massachusetts.

With no trains or other mechanical transportation, farmers who didn't live near the coast had to use carts and wagons to get their goods to market. Roads, if they existed at all in the countryside, were usually just narrow dirt trails. Farmers who lived near rivers such as the Connecticut and the Merrimack could transport crops on boats.

In some areas, land was expensive, such as in eastern Massachusetts, where all the best farmland was already taken. When owners sold land, they asked a high price. A family's sons received the family's land when the father died, but until then, it was under the father's control. Many young men worked in the cities or sought land in other colonies, instead of waiting to inherit their family's land. Some men had skills they had learned from their fathers, such as working with iron or wood. They could set up shops and save to buy land. A young man without skills might work for pay doing chores on someone else's farm. During wartime, men might join the military to make money. For most colonists, owning land was an important goal. Even wealthy merchants usually owned farms, although they had hired help to do the farm work.

Small Changes for Women

Most Massachusetts women of the 18th century continued to devote their lives to raising families and running the household. Yet some women did have new opportunities. A small but growing number of women ran their own businesses. Common jobs included sewing, preparing medicines, serving food, and running shops. Mary Crathorne of Boston advertised *"that upon timely notice, she can supply any person with . . . articles of mustard or chocolate."*

Tough Travels

Sarah Kemble Knight of Boston noted some of the problems of colonial travel in her 1704 diary. On a 250-mile (400-km) trip on horseback from Boston to New Haven, Connecticut, and back, she faced muddy roads and flooded rivers that she struggled to cross. Tree branches scratched her skin as she rode on narrow paths in the dark. She wrote that near the end of her journey, *"my horse dropped down under me as dead."*

Eighteenth-century Massachusetts saw small, but meaningful changes for women. Some took up less traditional work running their own business or working in occupations usually reserved for men. This drawing illustrates the female owner of a tinware shop showing her wares to a customer.

Some women also did jobs that were usually considered "man's work," such as working with metal. One Boston woman published an ad saying she could make "*tea-kettles and coffee pots, copper drinking pots, brass and copper sauce pans . . . and fish kettles.*" Women without skills or the money to open shops often hired themselves out as servants.

The women of the upper classes were expected to know how to arrange large feasts, keep their guests comfortable, and make their husbands look good. Their social events helped their husbands business relations and gave their families a chance to encourage marriages between their children.

The Great Awakening

Starting in the 1720s, some ministers in the Colonies began preaching about the evils of sin. They focused on a person's direct relation with God. These ministers wanted people to denounce their sins and declare their faith in Jesus Christ. The ministers preached at huge meetings called revivals. Their goal was to "awaken" people so they would follow Christ. By the 1740s, this movement was called The Great Awakening.

A Massachusetts minister named Jonathan Edwards played a large role in the Great Awakening. Edwards preached in Northampton and other Massachusetts towns along the Connecticut River. The revivals, he wrote, "*have brought [people] immediately to quit their sinful practices. . . . When once the Spirit of God began to be so wonderfully poured out in a general way through the town, people had soon done with their old quarrels . . . the tavern was soon left empty . . . and every day seemed in many respects like a Sabbath day.*"

By the 1750s, the Great Awakening lost steam in Massachusetts and the rest of the Colonies. People were no longer interested in the emotional style of speaking that ministers often used at revivals, and they began to return to their old churches. The Great Awakening left some lasting changes, however. Afterward, more people believed that they had worth as individuals: They didn't have to be Congregationalists to receive God's blessing—or to have

PROFILE

Phillis Wheatley

Around 1760, Phillis Wheatley was taken from West Africa and sold into slavery. She was just six or seven at the time. She ended up in Boston with a family that taught her how to read and write and encouraged her talents as a poet. In 1773, Wheatley became the first African American to publish a book of poetry. She was freed the next year. In one of her poems, she wrote about her experience as a slave and compared it to the colonists' lives under British rule.

I, young in life, by seeming cruel fate
Was snatch'd from Afric[a]'s fancy'd happy seat:...
Steel'd was the soul and no misery mov'd
That from a father seiz'd his babe belov'd:
Such, such my case. And can I then but pray
Others may never feel tyrannic sway?

political rights. The Great Awakening also boosted membership in other Protestant faiths. One Protestant group with Puritan roots, the Baptists, saw some growth in Massachusetts after the Great Awakening.

The Intellectual Life

During the 18th century, Massachusetts produced some of the best thinkers in America. Jonathan Edwards was one example. Edwards was an influential theologian and preacher. He read books by the best European writers of the day, and he accepted new scientific ideas. He tried to understand things in nature, such as rainbows, by exploring the science connected to them.

theologian—a scholar who writes about how people relate to God

At Harvard College, John Winthrop, a descendant of the first governor of Massachusetts Bay, taught the newest scientific theories to his students. Winthrop owned one of the few telescopes in America and opened the first laboratory in the Colonies to conduct physics experiments around 1754.

Books published in Massachusetts often featured the writings of clergymen, but nonreligious writings also appeared. Several authors wrote histories of the colony. Publishers also printed almanacs. These books had information on the night sky, weather, and planting and included poems and parts of articles from well-known writers.

Engrav'd Printed & Sold by PAUL RE

Birthplace of Revolution

IN AN ATTEMPT TO PROTECT THEIR RIGHTS, *Patriots in Boston lead the fight for American independence from Great Britain.*

Great Britain's victory in the French and Indian War vastly expanded its empire. The British took control of all of France's lands on the North American mainland. To pay its war debts and defend its new lands, the British government needed money. In 1764, Parliament passed the Sugar Act. The law called for tougher action against molasses smugglers and gave British warships the power to search American ships. Massachusetts merchants used molasses to make rum. They feared they would go out of business if they couldn't smuggle in molasses.

OPPOSITE: An engraving by Paul Revere of the Boston Massacre shows British soldiers firing on a crowd of civilians who had been taunting them with claims of unfair treatment by the British government.

In Boston, Samuel Adams led a protest against the Sugar Act. He said that because the colonists did not have any representatives to speak for them in Parliament, it was unfair for the British to impose taxes on them. Adams believed that the Sugar Act destroyed *"our . . . right to govern and tax ourselves. It strikes at our British privileges, which . . . we hold in common with our fellow-subjects who are natives of Britain."*

PROFILE

Samuel Adams

In Boston, Samuel Adams played a part in most of the protests against British policies in America. Adams came from a fairly wealthy family, but he had little interest in running the family businesses, which included malting, or turning barley into malt for beer. His true love was politics, and he believed that everyone had rights that could not be taken away. These *"natural"* rights, he wrote, were *"founded in the law of God and nature, and are the common rights of mankind."* One important right was self-government: People should freely come together and create a community and then govern themselves as they chose. Adams believed the British were trying to take that right away from the Americans.

VIOLENCE IN BOSTON

The next year, Parliament passed the Stamp Act. This law required the colonists to pay a tax whenever they used paper for public documents, newspapers, or even playing cards. In Boston, people who opposed the Stamp Act rioted in the streets. They tore down the house of the man who was supposed to collect the new tax and threatened to kill him. Two weeks later, they marched to the house of Lieutenant Governor Thomas Hutchinson. Governor Francis Bernard described the scene in a report to London: *"Everything movable was destroyed in the most minute manner except such things of value as were worth carrying off. . . ."*

Many of the protesters were members of the Sons of Liberty. This group actively fought British policies in the years before the American Revolution. Several other colonies had their own Sons of Liberty, and protests against the Stamp Act spread.

Patroits were among the people who opposed the Stamp Act. Patriots from Boston, such as Samuel Adams and James Otis, led the effort to unite the Colonies against the British. Representatives from nine colonies met in New York City at what was later called the Stamp Act Congress. They agreed that the Colonies should boycott British merchants. When the boycott began, British merchants quickly started losing money.

Patriot—a colonist who favored independence from England

They pressured Parliament to repeal the Stamp Act, and Parliament agreed.

Then in 1767, Parliament passed the Townshend Acts, which included new duties on tea, paper, and other items. The law also sent more British officials to Boston to fight colonial smuggling. Once again, Massachusetts began a boycott of British goods, which other colonies also joined.

boycott—an agreement made by a group of people to refuse to purchase goods from a nation or company

In 1768, British troops landed at Boston to keep order. The British troops wore long, red coats and were commonly known as "redcoats" or "lobsterbacks." The troops often questioned people as they walked at night, and some soldiers took jobs away from local men. (The soldiers worked when they were off duty to earn extra money.) Some soldiers committed crimes, as well.

Tensions finally exploded into violence. On March 5, 1770, British soldiers fired into a crowd that had been taunting them. Five American colonists died. The Sons of Liberty soon called the killings a massacre, hoping to stir up more hatred against the British. A local court ruled that the soldiers were not guilty of murder. To the Patriots, however, the Boston Massacre was another sign that the British threatened American safety and rights.

The Colonies began sharing ideas with each other through organizations called committees of correspondence. Samuel Adams created the first one in Boston in 1772.

Committee members discussed political ideas and then shared them with other committees across Massachusetts. From Massachusetts, the idea of creating committees of correspondence spread to other colonies. The committees kept in touch with each other within a single colony and between the different colonies.

The Boston MASSACRE

Captain Thomas Preston was the British officer who led the troops at what came to be called the Boston Massacre. He described the events of March 5, 1770:

. . . a general attack was made on the men by a great number of heavy clubs and snowballs being thrown at them, by which all our lives were in imminent danger, some persons at the same time from behind calling out, damn your bloods—why don't you fire. Instantly three or four of the soldiers fired, one after another, and directly after three more in the same confusion and hurry.

John Adams, the cousin of Samuel Adams, was the lead lawyer who defended Preston and the other accused soldiers. Even though Adams was a Patriot, he believed that everyone, including British soldiers, deserved a fair trial. Adams later became the second President of the United States.

A "TEA PARTY"

Around the time of the Boston Massacre, Parliament repealed most of the duties from the Townshend Acts. The only one that remained was on tea. People across the Colonies boycotted British tea. In 1773, the British hoped to encourage Americans to drink more tea by lowering its price. However, the duty remained in place, which still angered many Patriots.

On the night of December 16, Boston Patriots disguised as Indians raided three British ships in the harbor which held 342 chests of tea. The Patriots dumped the tea into Boston Harbor. George Hewes was one of the disguised Patriots that night. He later wrote, "*In about three hours from the time we went on board, we had thus broken and thrown overboard every tea chest to be found in the ship. . . .*

British officials reacted angrily to what the Patriots called the Boston Tea Party. Parliament passed several laws which the colonists called the Intolerable Acts. The laws closed down the port of Boston and placed a military governor in charge of Massachusetts.

During the spring of 1774, new British troops arrived in Boston. Lawmakers in New York and Virginia called for the American colonies to send representatives to a meeting. The representatives would discuss the situation in Massachusetts and how the Colonies should respond. Held in Philadelphia, Pennsylvania, in the fall, this meeting was called the First Continental Congress. The Colonies declared that Parliament had no right to tax them or control their politics without their approval.

War Comes to Massachusetts

By the end of 1774, the Patriots had set up their own illegal government within Massachusetts. They also gathered weapons and supplies. Across the colony, some towns formed special militia units called minutemen. The town leaders in Concord, Massachusetts, wrote that *"said company or companies [could] stand at a minute's warning in case of an alarm."*

minuteman—a member of the Patriot militia who was prepared to fight the British on a moment's notice

Few people talked about independence, however. Most residents of Massachusetts simply wanted to protect their rights as British subjects. Still, some people were starting to think that the Colonies would eventually have to break away from Great Britain. Only then could they enjoy their natural rights. The colonists believed these rights came from God and included the right to live without laws that placed unfair limits on freedom.

General Thomas Gage was now the governor of Massachusetts. He knew that the Patriots were gathering weapons. On the night of April 18, he sent troops out of Boston to nearby Concord to seize weapons stored there.

Paul Revere and William Dawes rode toward Concord to warn the citizens. They also alerted minutemen in Lexington, which was on the route to Concord. Revere was caught by the British before he reached Concord, but Dawes and another rider did make it there.

On April 19, the British troops reached Lexington. About 70 minutemen waited at the town green. John Parker, the colonists' captain, supposedly told his men, *"Don't fire unless fired upon, but if they mean to have a war, let it begin here."* Someone fired a shot—historians don't know for sure if he was British or American. The redcoats then began firing wildly at the colonists, and the minutemen fired back. When the shooting finally ended, eight Americans were dead. The British then marched on to Concord.

A 1775 colored engraving by Amos Doolittle shows British troops arriving in Concord after defeating minutemen stationed in Lexington.

A larger group of both minutemen and militia waited for the British at Concord. The two sides exchanged shots at a bridge near the town, and a few soldiers on both sides died. The bloodiest fighting came as the British retreated to Boston without seizing the weapons they had come for. The British totaled about 270 casualties, while the Americans had about 90. With the Battles of Lexington and Concord, the American Revolution had begun.

casualties—soldiers who are killed, wounded, captured, or missing during a battle

The Battle at Concord

William Emerson was a minister in Concord. He was also the grandfather of Ralph Waldo Emerson, one of America's greatest thinkers. In his diary, William Emerson described some of the fighting he saw on April 19, 1775:

The three companies of [British] troops soon quitted their post at the bridge and retreated in the greatest disorder and confusion to the main body. . . . In the meantime, a party of our men (150) took the back way through the Great Fields . . . and had placed themselves to advantage, lying in ambush behind walls, fences, and buildings, ready to fire upon the enemy on their retreat.

Revolution and Independence

As fighting continued in Massachusetts, colonial political leaders met in Philadelphia at the Second Continental Congress in May 1775. The other colonies agreed to form an army to help Massachusetts fight the British. At the same time, many of the representatives at the Congress still hoped that Americans could settle their differences with Great Britain.

For the next few months, the main fighting of the American Revolution took place in and around Boston. One major battle, the Battle of Bunker (Breeds) Hill, was won by the British, but they lost a large number of troops. The battle convinced the British that the Americans were serious about fighting for their rights.

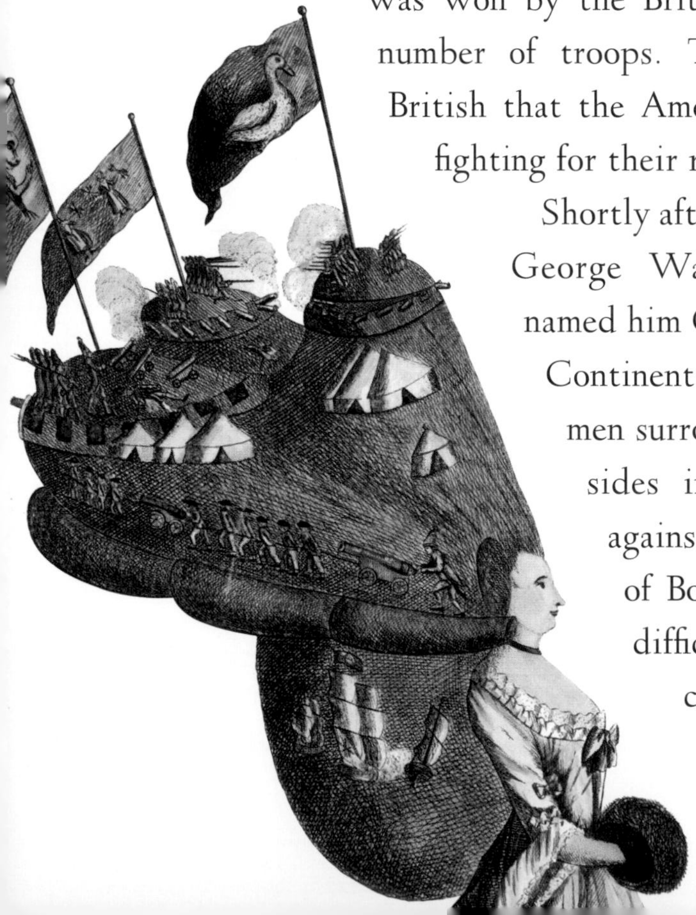

Shortly afterward, the Congress made George Washington a general and named him Commander-in-Chief of the Continental Army. For months, his men surrounded the British on three sides in Boston, trapping them against the sea. During the siege of Boston, the Patriots made it difficult to get supplies into the city, and many residents struggled to find food and fuel. The British stole what they wanted from the homes of people who had fled the city.

Some fighting took place during the fall and winter of 1775, but there were no major battles. The Americans lacked large guns to blast away at the enemy. Cannon finally arrived in January 1777. Rather than risk a major confrontation, the British decided to leave the besieged city in March. They sailed to Nova Scotia, a British port in what is now Canada. There they waited for reinforcements before heading to New York.

No more major battles took place in Massachusetts during the war. However, soldiers from Massachusetts still fought in other colonies, and the women left behind played an important role. They sewed clothes for the troops and filled in for their husbands, fathers, and sons on family farms. The war also gave African Americans, both slave and free, a chance to show their loyalty. In Massachusetts, several hundred slaves won their freedom by agreeing to fight for the Patriot cause. Some free African Americans also volunteered.

On land, the fighting moved into New York, while along the coast the British prepared to attack Charleston, South Carolina. On July 1, 1776, the members of the Continental Congress began to discuss the Declaration of Independence, just drafted by Thomas Jefferson of Virginia.

OPPOSITE: A satirical English engraving picturing the Battle of Bunker Hill worn as a head ornament by an Englishwoman.

John Adams spoke out on the need for independence. His words were not recorded, but Jefferson said that Adams's speech stirred the delegates to rise from their seats. The next day, the delegates voted for independence. Adams wrote to his wife Abigail, *"I am well aware of the toil, and blood, and treasure, that it will cost us to maintain this declaration. . . . Yet, through all the gloom, I can see the rays of . . . light and glory."* The final wording of the Declaration was approved on July 4th.

A 1765 portrait of John Hancock by John Singleton Copley.

John Hancock of Boston served as the president of the Congress. He had inherited a large fortune from his uncle, Thomas Hancock, and he generously supported the Patriot cause. In Philadelphia, he was the first representative to sign the Declaration of Independence. The other signers of the Declaration from Massachusetts were John and Samuel Adams, Robert Treat Paine, and Elbridge Gerry. The 13 Colonies were now the United States of America.

The State of Massachusetts

In November 1777, the Congress approved the Articles of Confederation. This document made the Congress the sole national government for the new nation. The Articles of Confederation took effect in 1781. Meanwhile, Massachusetts was creating its own state government.

constitution—the written set of guiding laws and principles for a government, state, or society

In late 1777 and early 1778, the General Court worked on a constitution. However, the towns rejected the constitution of 1778. In the court's proposal, only white men who owned property would have the right to vote. Some citizens disliked excluding African Americans and Indians from voting. Other towns did not like certain property requirements.

The next year, each town sent representatives to a convention to create a new state constitution. John and Samuel Adams played major roles in writing the new constitution. The convention approved this document, which created a government with three branches. The legislative branch, made up of two houses, would make laws. The executive branch, led by the governor, would carry out the laws. The judicial branch, or the courts, would make sure the laws were carried out fairly.

The new Massachusetts constitution took effect in October 1780. A year later, the last major battle of the

American Revolution was fought in Virginia. With aid from France, General Washington and his troops forced the British to surrender at Yorktown. The war officially ended in 1783, when British and American officials signed the Treaty of Paris.

The End of *Slavery*

Two lawsuits filed in 1781 challenged the legality of slavery in Massachusetts. One of these cases reached the state supreme court, the most powerful court in Massachusetts. In 1783, Chief Justice William Cushing wrote, "*The idea of slavery is inconsistent with our own conduct and constitution; and there can be no such thing as [slavery] of a rational creature.*" Cushing based his judgment on these words in the Massachusetts constitution: "*all men are born free and equal.*" Massachusetts became the first of the original 13 states to ban slavery.

A National Constitution

The United States now had its independence. However, the national government was weak under the Articles of Confederation, which let the states keep many powers. The national government couldn't force states to pay taxes, and it couldn't solve disputes between individual states.

In Massachusetts, one key issue was debt. Returning soldiers had been paid with paper money that was now worthless. They and other local residents owed money to local merchants. They also faced higher taxes. Massachusetts courts began seizing farmland from some debtors and selling it to pay for the owners' debts. Debtors without land were sent to jail. In some towns in western Massachusetts, residents struggling to pay debts protested the new taxes. In 1786, Daniel Shays, a captain during the American Revolution, led some protesters in a revolt. They marched on the federal arsenal at Springfield, Massachusetts, where they battled government troops. Fighting continued into 1787 before the state finally ended the revolt.

Across the United States, Shays's Rebellion stirred fears among the wealthy that the national government was too weak to end such revolts. Some political leaders called for a national convention to come up with a plan for a new form of government. In September 1787, representatives met in Philadelphia at the national Constitutional Convention. The representatives created a brand-new government, spelled out in the U.S. Constitution. The Massachusetts delegates who signed the Constitution were Nathaniel Gorham and Rufus King. On February 6, 1788, Massachusetts became the sixth state to ratify, or approve, the Constitution.

Since the founding of Plymouth, residents of Massachusetts had stressed self-rule. They valued freedom. They believed in creating documents that set limits on a government's power. Boston, because of its role in the American Revolution, has been called "the cradle of liberty." Many of the ideals and values that all Americans still share had their roots in the rocky soil of Massachusetts. ❋

Time Line

1602 Bartholomew Gosnold explores islands just off the coast of Massachusetts.

1620 The Pilgrims reach Plymouth.

1626 Puritan settlers from Cape Ann found Naumkeag, which is later renamed Salem.

1630 John Winthrop leads a large group of Puritans to Massachusetts. He is the first governor of the Massachusetts Bay Colony. Puritans found Shawmut, later renamed Boston.

1636 Puritans from Massachusetts and Connecticut unite to defeat the Pequot Indians. A college later named Harvard is founded in Cambridge.

1660 Parliament passes the first of several Navigation Acts, which threaten business interests in Massachusetts.

1675–1676
New Englanders battle the Wampanoag and other tribes in King Philip's War.

1677 Massachusetts Bay takes official control of Maine.

1684 King Charles II takes back the charter of Massachusetts Bay, giving him direct control over the colony.

1691 King William I combines Massachusetts Bay and Plymouth into one colony with a new charter.

1692 Dozens of people in Salem and surrounding towns are accused of witchcraft, and 20 people are executed.

1704 French and Indian forces raid Deerfield, in western Massachusetts, killing about 50 settlers.

1730s The minister Jonathan Edwards of Northampton helps spark the Great Awakening in Massachusetts.

1745 Militia from Massachusetts and the rest of New England, organized by Governor William Shirley, take the French fort of Louisbourg, on Cape Breton Island.

1755 During the French and Indian War, Governor William Shirley briefly serves as the commander of all British and American troops in North America.

1764 Samuel Adams and other Boston residents challenge the Sugar Act.

1765 Mobs in Boston violently protest the Stamp Act.

1768 British troops arrive in Boston to keep order.

1770 British soldiers kill five Boston residents in what the Patriots call the Boston Massacre.

1773 Patriots dump chests of tea into Boston harbor. This protest of British tax policies is called the Boston Tea Party.

1774 Parliament passes the Intolerable Acts, which send more troops to Boston and limit self-rule in Massachusetts; Massachusetts sends representatives to the First Continental Congress in Philadelphia; Britain closes Boston harbor.

1775 At Lexington and Concord, Patriots and British troops fight the first battles of the American Revolution.

1776 The British are forced to leave Boston. Samuel and John Adams argue for independence at the Second Continental Congress. John Hancock, as president of the Congress, is the first person to sign the Declaration of Independence.

1780 Massachusetts approves its state constitution.

1781 The Battle of Yorktown is the last major battle of the American Revolution.

1783 The Treaty of Paris officially ends the American Revolution and confirms American independence.

1787 At the Constitutional Convention in Philadelphia, Massachusetts representatives Rufus King and Nathaniel Gorham sign the U.S. Constitution.

1788 Massachusetts is the sixth state to ratify the Constitution.

Resources

BOOKS

Allen, Thomas B. *George Washington, Spymaster: How the Americans Outspied the British and Won the Revolutionary War*. Washington, D.C.: National Geographic, 2004.

Bullock, Steven C. *The American Revolution: A History in Documents*. New York: Oxford University Press, 2003.

Grace, Catherine O'Neill, and Margaret Bruchac. *1621: A New Look at the First Thanksgiving*. Washington, D.C.: National Geographic, 2001.

Harness, Cheryl. *The Revolutionary John Adams*. Washington, D.C.: National Geographic, 2003.

Moe, Barbara. *The Charter of the Massachusetts Bay Colony: A Primary Source Investigation of the 1629 Charter*. New York: Rosen Primary Source, 2003.

Slavicek, Louis Chipley. *Life Among the Puritans*. San Diego: Lucent Books, 2001.

Wood, Peter. *Strange New Land: African Americans, 1617–1776*. New York: Oxford University Press, 1996.

WEB SITES

The American Colonist's Library: A Treasury of Primary Source Documents
http://www2.pitnet.net/primarysources/
This Web site has links to documents from the colonial era, including many relating to Massachusetts.

Boston Massacre Historical Society
http://www.bostonmassacre.net/
This site provides a detailed look at the massacre and the events before and afterward.

The Library of Congress Presents America's Story from America's Library
http://www.americaslibrary.gov/cgi-bin/page.cgi
The Library of Congress's Web page for kids contains fascinating information on Massachusetts and other American colonies.

Mass.gov Interactive Statehouse
http://www.mass.gov/statehouse/
This site from the state of Massachusetts has several features on colonial history.

National Park Service-Boston African-American National Historic Site
http://www.nps.gov/boaf/slaveryinboston.htm
This site from the National Park Service traces the history of slavery in Boston.

Plimoth Plantation
http://www.plimoth.org
This is the official site for the "living history museum" devoted to life in Plymouth colony.

Representative Poetry Online-Anne Bradstreet: To My Dear and Loving Husband
http://eir.library.utoronto.ca/rpo/display/poem217.html
This site has the complete text of Anne Bradstreet's 17th-century poem.

University of Missouri-Kansas City School of Law-Famous American Trials: Salem Witchcraft Trials 1692
http://www.law.umkc.edu/faculty/projects/ftrials/salem/salem.htm
A detailed account of the trials can be found at this site, including testimony from accused witches and their accusers.

Quote Sources

CHAPTER ONE

p. 14 "as healthful a climate." http://wyllie.lib.virginia.edu:8086/perl/toccer-new?id=J1006.xml&images=images/modeng&data=/texts/english/modeng/parsed&tag=public&part=all. Gosnold, Bartholomew. *Master Bartholomew Gosnold's Letter to his Father, touching his first voyage to Virginia, 1602*; p. 15 "The ground is so fertile." *Annals of America, Volume 1*. Chicago: Encyclopedia Britannica, 1968, p. 36; p. 17 "clapped in prison." Miller, Perry, ed. *The American Puritans*. Garden City, N.Y.: Anchor, 1956, p. 6; p. 17 "separated . . . from all." http://www.pilgrimhall.org/PSNoteNewReligiousControversies.htm. Maxwell, Richard Howland. *Religious Controversies in Plymouth Colony*. Pilgrim Society Note, Series Two, June 1996; p. 18 "dangerous shoals." Miller, p. 16; p. 19 "were not a little." Miller, p. 16; p. 21 "became a special." *Annals of America, Volume 1*, p. 67; p. 22 "[William Bradford] sent." http://www.nationalcenter.org/Pilgrims.html. Winslow, Governor Edward. *How the Pilgrims Lived*, 1621.

CHAPTER TWO

p. 26 "When they came ashore." Miller, Perry, ed. *The American Puritans*. Garden City, N.Y.: Anchor, 1956, p. 18; p. 27 "We, whose names." *Annals of America, Volume 1*. Chicago: Encyclopedia Britannica, 1968, p. 64; p. 30 "The laws of the civil." Garrett, John. *Roger Williams*. New York: Macmillan, 1970, p. 186; p. 31 "for those who have." http://www.harvardmagazine.com/on-line/1102194.html. Gomes, Peter G. "Anne Hutchinson—Brief life of Harvard's 'midwife': 1595–1643." *Harvard Magazine*, November–December 2002; p. 35 "It was a fearful." *Annals of America, Volume 1*, p. 83.

CHAPTER THREE

p. 38 "the poorest person." Taylor, Alan. *American Colonies*. New York: Penguin Books, 2001, p. 172; p. 42 "[God] took away." Miller, Perry, ed. *The American Puritans*. Garden City, N.Y.: Anchor, 1956, p. 229; p. 43 "all youths and maids." Axtell, James, ed. *The American People in Colonial New England*. West Haven, Conn.: Pendulum Press, 1973, p. 142; p. 45 "one chief project." *Annals of America, Volume 1*. Chicago: Encyclopedia Britannica, 1968, p. 184; p. 46 "great dishonor of God." http://masstraveljournal.com/features/1101chrisban.html. Danko, C., 2001–2004; p. 47 "played with their bare." Dunton, John. *Letters Written from New England*. New York: Burt Franklin, 1967, p. 285; p. 47 "I prize thy love." Miller, p. 272.

CHAPTER FOUR

p. 54 "we traveled about half." http://www.gutenberg.org/dirs/etext97/crmmr10.txt. Rowlandson, Mary. *Captivity and Restoration*; p. 55 "The king can in reason." http://www.publicbookshelf.com/public_html/Our_Country_Vol_1/historyco_ia.html. LoveToKnow Corporation, 2000; p. 57 "for your own safety." *Annals of America, Volume 1*. Chicago: Encyclopedia Britannica, 1968, p. 278; p. 58 "did but look." http://wyllie.lib.virginia.edu:8086/perl/toccer-new?id=BoySal1.sgm&images=images/modeng&data=/texts/english/modeng/oldsalem&tag=public&part=71&division=div2. Boyer, Paul, and Stephen Nissenbaum, eds. *The Salem witchcraft papers, Volume 1: verbatim transcripts of the legal documents of the Salem witchcraft outbreak of 1692*.

CHAPTER FIVE

p. 62 "have served . . . faithfully." Morgan, Edmund S. *The Genuine Article*. New York: W.W. Norton and Company, 2004, p. 119; p. 62 "blackish and blue" and "all his back." Demos, John. *A Little Commonwealth: Family Life in Plymouth Colony, Second Edition*. New York: Oxford University Press, 2000, p. 114; p. 63 "my well-beloved friend." Demos, p. 117; p. 63 "at the public charge." Morgan, p. 114; p. 64 "lawful captives." Morgan, p. 111; pp. 66–67 "can do all sorts." Towner, Lawrence W. *A Good Master Well Served: Masters and Servants in Colonial Massachusetts, 1620–1750*. New York: Garland Publishing, 1998, p. 109; p. 67 "The efforts made." Library of Congress Printed Ephemera Collection, Portfolio 37, Folder 16. *Petition for Freedom by Massachusetts Slaves*. Boston: April 20, 1773.

CHAPTER SIX

p. 71 "not long before." http://www.memorialhall.mass.edu/classroom/curriculum_6th/lesson5/resources/L00_068_06.html. Williams, Rev. John. *The Redeemed Captive Returning to Zion*, 1774, p. 6; p. 72 "saluted us with." Leckie, Robert. *The Wars of America*. New York: Harper and Row, 1981, p. 35; p. 72 "Never was a place." Parkman, Francis. *A Half-Century of Conflict, Volume 2*, 1892; p. 76 "We had no other." Anderson, Fred. *A People's Army: Massachusetts Soldiers and Society in the Seven Years' War*. New York: W.W. Norton and Company, 1984, p. 73; p. 77 "most destructive of English." *Annals of America, Volume 2*. Chicago: Encyclopedia Britannica, 1968, p. 74.

CHAPTER SEVEN

p. 81 "the persons concerned." *Annals of America, Volume 1*. Chicago: Encyclopedia Britannica, 1968, p. 455; p. 83 "that upon timely notice." Moynihan, Ruth Barnes, et al, eds. *Second to None: A Documentary History of American Women, Volume 1*. Lincoln: University of Nebraska Press, 1993, p. 116; p. 83 "my horse dropped." Knight, Sarah Kemble. *The Journal of Madam Knight*. Boston: David R. Godine, 1972, p. 38; p. 84 "tea-kettles and coffee pots." De Pauw, Linda Grant. *Founding Mothers: Women in America in the Revolutionary Era*. Boston: Houghton Mifflin, 1975, p. 33; p. 85 "have brought [people]." http://www.mnvbc.org/articles/edwards_conversions.html. Edwards, Jonathan. *Conversions: Manner of conversion various*; p. 86 "I, young in life." Moynihan, p. 158.

CHAPTER EIGHT

p. 90 "our . . . right to govern." Wells, William V. The Life and Public Services of Samuel Adams, Volume 1. Freeport, N.Y.: Books for Libraries Press, 1969, p. 48; p. 90 "founded in the law." Wells, p. 23; p. 91 "Everything movable was destroyed." *Annals of America, Volume 2*. Chicago: Encyclopedia Britannica, 1968, pp. 150–151; p. 93 "a general attack." http://www.law.umkc.edu/faculty/projects/ftrials/bostonmassacre/prestonaccount2.html. Jensen, Merrill, ed. English Historical Documents, Volume IX. London, 1964, pp. 750–753; p. 94 "In about three hours." http://historymatters.gmu.edu/d/5799/. Hewes, George Robert Twelve. A Shoemaker and the Tea Party. Hawkes, James. A Retrospect of the Boston Tea Party. New York: 1834, pp. 36–41; p. 95 "said company or companies." Gross, Robert A. The Minutemen and Their World. New York: Hill and Wang, 1976, p. 59; p. 96 "Don't fire unless." http://www.memory.loc.gov/ammem/today/jul13/html. p. 59; p. 97 "The three companies." Commager, Henry Steele, and Richard B. Morris, eds. The Spirit of 'Seventy-Six. New York: Harper and Row, 1967, p. 85; p. 100 "I am well aware." Annals of America, Volume 2, p. 431; p. 102 "The idea of slavery." http://www.pbs.org/wgbh/aia/part2/2h38t.html. Blaustein, Albert P., and Robert L. Zangrando, eds. Civil Rights and the Black American: A Documentary History. Washington Square Press, 1968; p. 102 "all men are born." http://www.mass.gov/legis/const.htm. Constitution of the Commonwealth of Massachusetts.

INDEX

About the Author and Consultant

MICHAEL BURGAN has has been writing about colonial America, religion, famous Americans, sports and many other subjects for children and young adults for more than 10 years. His work has been published in *The New York Times, in Sports Illustrated for Kids,* and by National Geographic. A former writer for Weekly Reader Corporation, Burgan has produced educational materials to be used by teachers in the classroom, as well. He is also a playwright and currently lives in Chicago.

BRENDAN McCONVILLE is currently a professor in the Department of History at Boston University where he teaches courses on colonial America, the American Revolution, and American Politics. He received his Ph.D. from Brown University. McConville has written numerous books and articles on the early years of the American colonies. He is also the consultant for the volumes on New Jersey, Connecticut, and Rhode Island in the *Voices from Colonial America* series. He lives in Boston.

Illustration Credits

Cover, pages 9, 29, 36, 40, 43, 51, 59, 60, 64, 78, 84, 88, 90, 96, 98, 100:
The Granger Collection

End sheets, pages 8, 86:
The Library of Congress

Title page, pages 53, 63, 73:
Picture Collection, The Branch Libraries, The New York Public Library

Pages 11, 24:
© Bettmann/CORBIS

Pages 12, 47:
The Getty Collection

Pages 21, 32, 68, 75:
© National Geographic Society

Pages 23, 32, 80:
American Antquarian Society

Page 34:
North Wind Picture Archives

Page 48:
Bridgeman Art Library

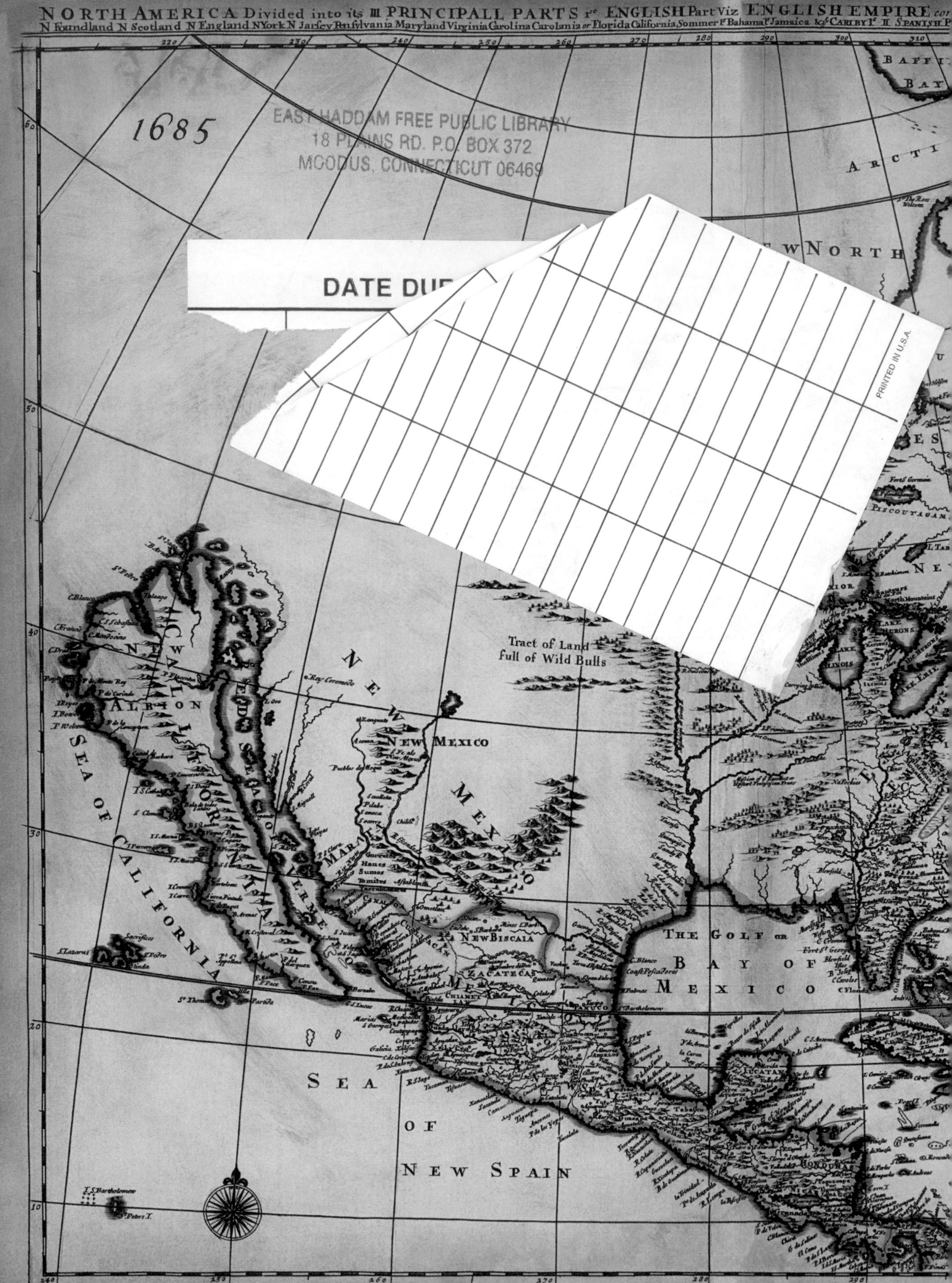
NORTH AMERICA Divided into its III PRINCIPALL PARTS
1685
NEW ALBION
SEA OF CALIFORNIA
NEW MEXICO
Tract of Land full of Wild Bulls
THE GOLF OR BAY OF MEXICO
NEW BISCAIA
SEA OF NEW SPAIN
DATE DUE
PRINTED IN U.S.A.